N

KEY

0	20	40	60	80	100	miles
0 20 40 60 80 100 120 140 160 Km			

1	LONGSIDE (LENABO)	21	SLINDON
2	AULDBAR	22	FARNBOROUGH
3	EAST FORTUNE (DREM)	23	MORETON
4	CHATHILL	24	TOLLER
5	CRAMLINGTON	25	LAIRA
6	KIRKLEATHAM	26	MULLION
7	BARLOW	27	TRESCO (SCILLY)
8	HOWDEN	28	BUDE
9	CRANWELL (training)	29	PEMBROKE
10	PULHAM	30	ANGLESEY
11	CARDINGTON	31	KILLEAGH
12	WORMWOOD SCRUBS	32	MALAHIDE
13	KINGSNORTH	33	WEXFORD
14	GODMERSHAM PARK	34	BARROW
15	WITTERSHAM	35	LARNE
16	POLEGATE	36	LOUGH NEAGH
17	CAPEL (FOLKESTONE)	37	DOAGH ISLAND
18	BOULOGNE	38	MACHRIHANISH
19	MARQUISE	39	SLINDON
20	INCHINNAN	40	LUCE BAY
		41	RAMSEY

◆ Mooring out stations
□ Uncompleted
✳ Constructional facility

THE BRITISH AIRSHIP
AT WAR, 1914–1918

Overleaf: Most numerous type of airship in service during the war was the SS Zero, which built up an impressive record. Here SSZ.3, one of the first SS Zero airships to enter service, is walked across the airfield by a handling party. SSZ.3 was stationed in turn at Pulham, Capel and East Fortune and flew 269 hours in service before being deleted in December, 1918.

Imperial War Museum

THE BRITISH AIRSHIP
AT WAR, 1914–1918

by

Patrick Abbott

TERENCE DALTON LIMITED
LAVENHAM . SUFFOLK
1989

Published by
TERENCE DALTON LIMITED

ISBN 0 86138 073 8

Text photoset in 10/12pt Baskerville

Printed in Great Britain at
The Lavenham Press Limited, Lavenham, Suffolk

Contents

To all the children, parents
and staff of St Paul's School,
Shepton Mallet

Above: The coastal airship C.27 is hauled down by a landing party at Pulham using a snatch block, as described on page 10. This airship was one of two Coastals from the same station shot down by German seaplanes in 1917.

Fleet Air Arm Museum

Right: The crew of the Coastal airship C.9, which had an outstanding career operating from Mullion in Cornwall. Left to right, W/T operator Ellis, Flight Lieutenant J. G. Struthers, Engineer Soames, Flight Sub-Lieutenant A. C. Jelf, Petty Officer Coxswain French.

Fleet Air Arm Museum

Preface

LIKE most writers of history, I am very much aware of my debt to the authors who have preceded me. Those who have helped me most are listed in the bibliography at the end of the book. In addition to their writings, I have used many contemporary records, which are also listed. These have enabled me to produce, in the second appendix, what I believe to be the first complete list of all the British airships commissioned during the Great War; a matter which has often been the subject of considerable inaccuracy.

I am indebted to various institutions whose officials have been generous in providing help with information, photocopies of documents or illustrations.

Experiments with the use of parachutes for escaping from airships were carried out at Pulham. In this photograph a number of the dummies used can be seen hanging from the car of C.17, the parachutes being housed in tubes fastened above the car. By a tragic irony, no member of the crew was able to escape when C.17 was shot down by German seaplanes on 21st April, 1917.

Fleet Air Arm Museum

The prototype of the Coastal Star class, C*1, whose car was taken from C.12 before being modified and improved. Based at East Fortune, C*1 flew 868 hours in service, more than any other airship of her class. The air delivery duct was placed externally on C*1 but was moved inside on later airships to improve the streamlining. *Fleet Air Arm Museum*

Among these are the Public Record Office, the Royal Aeronautical Society, the Imperial War Museum, the Royal Air Force Museum, the Fleet Air Arm Museum, the Scottish Museum of Flight and the Bristol Reference Library.

I would particularly like to thank Anthony Gorst and Norman Peake for their suggestions and help. I must also express my indebtedness to my publishers and their editor, Robert Malster, whose interest and knowledge have added greatly to any value the book may have.

Finally, I would like to express my admiration of the men who flew in airships. They have nearly all gone by now, but if this book helps to keep them in memory it will have been worthwhile.

Patrick Abbott
January, 1989

CHAPTER ONE

The Hunter

WEDNESDAY, 3rd October, 1917, was a clear day, but very windy, so the stubby and ungainly bulk of the airship C.9 wallowed and dipped as she escorted a convoy down the English Channel, some twenty miles south of Plymouth.

Flying low above the waves to windward of the vessels, she matched her speed to that of the destroyers steaming below her, keeping careful watch and always ready to swoop into action at any sign of the German U-boats it was her business to detect, deter or destroy. As on numerous previous patrols, the five men in her crew had to contend not only with danger but also with cold, cramp, intolerable engine roar and the boredom of long periods of inactivity.

The airship's captain, Flight Lieutenant J. Struthers, was a renowned submarine hunter whose luck was a byword in the Airship Service. His success was not entirely due to luck, however; his enthusiasm created its own opportunities by keeping a primitive aircraft and her crew flying to the limits of their endurance for many hours at a time, day after day and month after month.

As the convoy crawled slowly westward over a choppy sea another group of vessels appeared over the horizon, moving northwards. Flight Lieutenant Struthers radioed to a nearby sister airship, C.23A, ordering her to take over charge of the westbound convoy, while C.9 herself moved across to escort the newcomers, a cruiser and two destroyers. Without incident or alarm, the ships soon reached the Eddystone lighthouse and passed beyond, making towards Plymouth and safety, with the airship still keeping guard overhead. From their cramped cockpits the crew could see, stretching far out to the southern horizon, the narrow space of sea where Britain's merchantmen and warships were at this time most busy and most threatened.

Reaching the end of his patrol and satisfied that there was no longer any danger, Flight Lieutenant Struthers turned the airship westward to make her way back to her base at Mullion. As she turned, her engineer looked backward over his shoulder to the east, where at the limit of visibility another convoy could be seen rounding Start Point.

Now the crew's long tedium of watching and waiting ended abruptly, for

Flight Lieutenant J. G. Struthers and his crew in the Coastal airship C.9, based at Mullion in Cornwall.
Fleet Air Arm Museum

1

from the middle of the group of ships came a towering spout of water. At once, C.9 was swung round and headed towards the torpedoed vessel, her two engines howling out their full power and the wind at her tail pushing her to a speed of around 90 mph. So quickly did the airship reach the convoy that the foamy track of the torpedo could still be discerned, stretching away from the stricken steamer. Flight Lieutenant Struthers turned his airship and followed the trail back to where the blurred shape of a submarine, invisible to the lookouts in the ships of the convoy, could be faintly seen from above. Balancing the thrust of her engines against the force of the gale, C.9 slowed to a stop and hovered momentarily before dropping her entire load of four small bombs on to the U-boat.

The airship leapt upwards at the sudden loss of weight. Almost immediately there came a muffled explosion underwater, bringing bubbles frothing to the surface. The wireless operator signalled by Aldis lamp for patrol ships from the convoy to join in the attack, and an armed trawler raced across to add her own onslaught of depth charges. Within minutes more bubbles and oil came flooding up from below, a sure sign that the U-boat had been badly damaged, if not destroyed.

But C.9 could not wait for confirmation. With very little fuel left in her tanks, she once more turned to make her way home. The possibility of disaster

was now close, for the headwind slowed the airship considerably and the forty-mile return flight to Mullion took six hours, with C.9 butting against a gale that forced her sometimes almost to a halt. When the exhausted crew finally brought their airship in to land there was fuel left for barely another half-hour.

This episode epitomizes the work of the Airship Service during the Great War: a few minutes of excitement and activity circled by countless hours of monotony, hazard, discomfort and cold. Many of the British airships saw no action at all, but each one contributed in some way to the fight against the greatest threat of the whole war to Britain's survival, that presented by German submarines in their efforts to destroy the shipping upon which this country depended for raw materials and food.

The true extent of the danger was never revealed to the general public, but the Government was fully aware of the threat and the Admiralty sought many and varied methods to combat this menace. Of these, the most inspired as well as the least publicised was probably the use of airships. Official policy during the war decreed that no details of airship construction or activity should be revealed, and a cloak of secrecy, much of it quite unnecessary, prevented the men of the Airship Service from receiving the credit to which they were undoubtedly entitled.

During four years of war the airship crews gave invaluable service to their

Opposite page: Seen here in the hands of the landing party, C.23A was commissioned in September, 1917, as a replacement for C.23. In eight months' service at Mullion she flew 900 hours before being wrecked at sea on 10th May, 1918, with the loss of one member of her crew.
Imperial War Museum

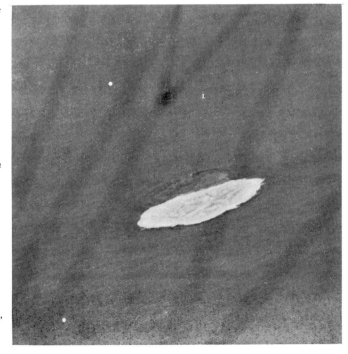

Right: A bomb bursting over a submerged U-boat, seen from the attacking airship.

country, and throughout that time it was the fight against the U-boats which preoccupied them above all else. In August, 1914, Britain possessed only seven military airships, all owned by the Admiralty. In the next four years another 225 were delivered, of which one was not accepted and 24 were sold to the Allies. By the time of the Armistice 100 had been scrapped, destroyed or lost in other ways, while 107 were still in commission. In 1914 and 1915 the airships flew a total of around 3,000 hours; in 1916, as their numbers increased, it was 7,000; in 1917 it jumped to 22,000; and in 1918, when Allied shipping losses were reduced to less than half those of the previous year, the figure was 56,000 hours. This makes a total of about 88,000 hours of flying, or more than two million miles flown, during the whole war. Almost incredibly, this was accomplished for a total loss of only forty-eight lives from all causes.

More detailed figures are available for the busiest and fiercest part of the campaign, from June, 1917, to October, 1918, inclusive. In every month of this

A North Sea airship returning to her base at Pulham in Norfolk after a patrol. *Mrs M. Martin*

period an average of fifty-six airships were on duty and in total they carried out 9,059 patrols averaging 6 hours 17 minutes each. Altogether, they flew 59,703 hours, made 2,210 escorts, sighted 134 mines, of which they destroyed seventy-three, and sighted forty-nine U-boats, attacking twenty-one of these with other help and six alone.

The figures do not tell the whole story, however, for it was the deterrent value of the airship operations which counted for most. It is alleged that the log of one captured German submarine was found to contain the laconic but illuminating entry: "Sighted airship—submerged."

One single statistic explains how the balance was tipped in favour of Britain: during the whole of the war, except for a single occasion, no ship escorted by an airship was ever sunk. Only when distance, weather or chance removed such protection were the U-boats able to close in for the kill. This meant that the war at sea was lost, however narrowly, by the Germans, and with it they lost the chance to starve Britain into defeat.

The British airships did not win the war by themselves, but without them the war might never have been won.

CHAPTER TWO

Historical, Technical and Operational Background

T HE STORY of the British airships did not start suddenly at the outbreak of war, and to understand what they and the men who flew them accomplished it is necessary to go back briefly to the very beginnings.

The history of the dirigible balloon or airship is almost as old as that of the balloon itself, since the first plans for such an aircraft were drawn up by a Frenchman, Jean Meusnier, early in 1784, only a few months after the Montgolfier brothers and J. A. C. Charles had built the world's first hot air and gas balloons. For want of a suitable prime mover, Meusnier's fish-shaped aircraft—had it ever been built—could never have flown effectively, and it was this crucial handicap which held up development for so long. During the early nineteenth century airships of various kinds were proposed, designed and even built. Some were fairly sophisticated in concept, others quite primitive, but all were prevented from being successful by the lack of a light yet powerful engine.

In 1852 Henri Giffard's airship flew about seventeen miles, powered by a lightweight steam engine, but it could move at less than six miles an hour and so was helpless in the teeth of even the mildest wind.

In 1884 two more Frenchmen, Renard and Krebs, built a very advanced airship powered by an electric motor. It became the first aircraft of any type to fly around a course and return safely to its starting point, but it was still badly underpowered and therefore too slow to warrant further development.

Eventually, in the same way that the discovery of hydrogen had made the gas balloon possible, the invention of the internal combustion engine at last made the airship a practicable proposition. One Karl Wolfert, a German, was the first man to fit such a power source to a dirigible—or, indeed, to any aircraft—and the early flights were promising. Unhappily, the primitive open burner which provided the ignition finally caused a fatal explosion, destroying both the craft and its inventor, in 1897.

With the coming of a much safer ignition system not long afterwards the way was clear for a fully successful airship to be at last constructed, and the honour of achieving this belongs to the Brazilian, Alberto Santos Dumont. His succession of small dirigibles, built from 1898 onwards, proved to be manoeuvrable, safe, reliable and reasonably fast. He made many memorable

Smallest of Santos Dumont's fourteen airships was his No 9 in which he once flew along the Champs Elysées and around the Arc de Triomphe. In this airship in 1903 Aida d'Acosta became the first and only woman to pilot an airship alone and unaccompanied.   *Musée de l'Air*

flights, of which the most famous is probably that which won him the Deutsch prize in 1901, when he flew from St Cloud to the Eiffel Tower and back.

The basic principles of airship design were now widely understood, and with the example of Santos Dumont to encourage them pioneers in many countries began to build small airships. Nearly all of these used a fabric envelope or gasbag which was kept firm and in streamlined shape by means of one or more internal bags, called ballonets, into which air was pumped as required to maintain the internal pressure.

A car—sometimes called a gondola—accommodated the engine, crew and equipment, and was slung beneath the gasbag by long suspension lines which distributed the weight evenly. As the efficiency of these lines depended upon their being at not too great an angle from the vertical, the car was perforce either very long or was slung well beneath the envelope.

Some means of regulating the trim was also common to these dirigibles:

either there was means of moving the centre of gravity or the dynamic action of horizontal rudders, termed elevators, was employed. The amount of lift could be adjusted either by valving gas or by releasing ballast, usually water. These near-universal features were not new and had been used by many of the early pioneers—the invention of the ballonet, indeed, is attributed to Meusnier—but until the advent of a suitable power source they had been of no more than academic interest. Together they helped to create the basic pattern of the typical non-rigid airship or "blimp", and many variations on the same simple theme appeared during the first decade of the twentieth century.

It was soon apparent that so far as airships were concerned mathematical reasons dictated that greater size brought greater efficiency. As a given shape becomes larger, so surface area increases as the square of the linear dimensions, whereas volume increases as the cube. A dirigible 300 feet long, for example, has nine times the surface area and therefore nine times the drag of one that is only 100 feet long, but it has twenty-seven times the volume and therefore twenty-seven times the lift. Unfortunately, there are practical limits to the size a non-rigid envelope, maintained in shape only by internal pressure, can attain. In order to overcome this handicap to unrestricted growth, two other forms of airship soon appeared.

The first of these was the semi-rigid, pioneered almost entirely by the French and the Italians. These craft used gasbags similar to those of non-rigids, but incorporated in them were rigid or partially flexible keels which helped to retain a firm and streamlined shape.

The second was the rigid airship, developed almost entirely by one man, Count Ferdinand von Zeppelin of Germany. His enormous creations, often referred to simply by the name of their originator, consisted essentially of an ultralight framework of aluminium—later duralumin—girders. This skeletal shape was covered by light fabric and to it were attached engines, cars and control surfaces. Inside were a score or so of separate compartments, each containing its own huge drum-shaped gasbag. However much the gas pressure varied, or even if one or two of the gasbags became completely deflated, Zeppelins could remain aloft safely and with their aerodynamic profile unaltered. These giant aircraft were the most advanced of all lighter-than-air flying machines, and many contemporary observers believed them to be potentially superior to all other forms of aircraft, in war as well as in peace.

Despite these differences the three types of airship, from whatever country or designer, had certain inescapable features in common. All used hydrogen as the medium of lift, partly because it is the lightest of gases and partly because, of only two alternatives, coal gas was too inefficient and helium was for many years far too rare and expensive. Hydrogen, readily produced and stored in cylinders, weighs about 5 lb for 1,000 cubic feet, as against normal air which weighs around 76 lb for the same volume at sea level (much depends upon altitude and pressure). The amount of lift depends upon the weight of air displaced, minus the weight of the gas displacing it, so it is evident that 1,000 cubic feet of hydrogen produces a gross lift of about 71 lb or, in realistic terms, 32,000 cubic feet give a gross lift of about one ton. Unfortunately, hydrogen, unlike helium, possesses the great defect of being highly inflammable, and when mixed with air is explosive.

As an airship ascends, the air pressure decreases, so allowing the gas inside the envelope to expand. When further expansion is impossible, the "pressure height" is reached and the gas escapes through automatic valves. Thereafter the rate of climb slackens, and at the "gas ceiling" ceases entirely.

Other factors govern airship flight even today and have to be allowed for.

Few of the earlier wartime airships had so effective an enclosed cabin as the Parseval HMA No 5, built by Vickers to a pre-war German design. She was delivered late in 1917 and served for less than a year.   *Norman Peake*

Hydrogen reacts to ambient conditions rather more quickly than does air, and so sunlight can cause "superheating", an effect also in evidence if an area of cold air is encountered suddenly. The gas is of a higher temperature than the surrounding air and so causes the temporary phenomenon of "false lift", which can be helpful or dangerous, depending upon circumstances. The opposite effect is experienced when a region of warm air is met, causing an abrupt loss of lift.

In addition to the gross static lift of the gas, from which is subtracted the weight of the airship's structure to obtain the amount of "disposable lift", a very different but quite appreciable source of lift is available to all dirigibles. This is gained by trimming the airship to fly at a slight nose-up angle, so that not only is the thrust of the propellers directed partly downwards but the whole envelope then acts like an aeroplane's wing and gives "dynamic lift", equivalent to perhaps a tenth of the static lift. The reverse effect is also obtainable with a nose-down attitude, so that airships can not only maintain the desired altitude for long periods without sacrificing gas or ballast but they can also dive and climb similarly. It follows that not only can an airship stall like an aeroplane, but also that it may stall upwards under certain conditions.

Another feature common to all airships and in sharp contrast to aeroplanes was the need for a numerous ground crew at both the beginning and the end of a flight. With dirigibles of all types and all countries the prescribed drill became very uniform. The airship was prepared in its hangar, then surrounded by the handling party of well-drilled helpers and "walked out", held, carried and restrained by their combined weight.

Out in the open, the airship was swung round to face into the wind and "eased up" on the handling guys, which were ropes attached either permanently to the structure or temporarily looped round suitable protuberances. In the former case the guys often ended in loops, through which members of the ground crew could pass their own lines as extensions. In this position, floating at just about head height above the ground, it was possible to "ballast up", in the English phrase, or "weigh off", which meant adjusting the buoyancy by carefully taking on or releasing ballast. The amount of lift was tested and measured by the number of men whose combined weight, pulling directly on the airship, could bring it down. Once the correct buoyancy was achieved the engines were started, all ropes were released in unison and the flight commenced.

When the flight ended, it was sometimes possible for the pilot to "ballast up" and adjust the trim before flying the airship very slowly upwind at a low height towards the landing party, who would attach their lines to the handling guys, take hold of the car and walk the craft back into the hangar. In difficult conditions or in gusty weather, however, such a simple procedure was not possible and it became necessary to drop a long and heavy trail rope, which was grabbed by the handling party, who then pulled the still-buoyant airship down within reach. Sometimes a loop of the trail rope was passed under the wheel of a "snatch block"—a form of swivelling pulley open at one side and set in concrete—in order to prevent the handlers from being lifted off their feet and to enable them to use their strength more efficiently.

The airships of the early twentieth century are often compared unfavourably with contemporary aeroplanes, but this is an unfair judgement and is based on the evidence of later developments and on hindsight. In fact for many years airships often excelled aeroplanes in certain important respects. Most airships could carry a considerable load of fuel and so remain aloft for many hours and cover long distances. They could also carry a large payload of cargo, bombs or guns, if required. Aeroplanes, by contrast, could usually lift only a small quantity of fuel, cargo or armament and this limited their practical use in both peace and war. An engine failure in an aeroplane, a not uncommon occurrence, meant an immediate and possibly hazardous descent, whereas airships in the same predicament could remain aloft and even carry out running repairs.

At this early period airships could not only reach higher altitudes than could most aeroplanes but often did so much faster. By dropping ballast and using full dynamic lift, many wartime Zeppelins escaped pursuing aeroplanes and left them toiling far below.

Even if pure speed in level flight is taken as the main criterion, the contrast between early airships and aeroplanes is still not overwhelmingly in favour of the latter, in the way it has undoubtedly become since. No airship of any era, it is true, has ever reached even 100 mph, and most have been much slower, but in the first decade of this century they frequently reached speeds approaching 50 mph, at a time when most aeroplanes could still not exceed 60 mph. The difference was not crucial for many purposes, and indeed the ability of airships to fly very slowly when required, or even to hover, made them far more suitable than aeroplanes for many tasks. That same ability also enabled them to fly at night or in fog, when aeroplanes were usually helpless.

All of this had become generally accepted wisdom in the years leading up to 1914. France, Germany and most other European countries believed that the airship, in one form or another, possessed great potential as a weapon of war. Development proceeded apace and Great Britain, entering the field somewhat belatedly, was determined not to be found wanting.

CHAPTER THREE

Pre-war British Airships

FOR MANY years Britain had lagged behind her continental neighbours in the development of all forms of aircraft. Ballooning, it is true, had long been a popular upper-class hobby and observation balloons had been used by the Royal Engineers in the Boer War and several colonial campaigns, but the first dirigible balloon built in this country did not appear until 1902. Constructed by Stanley Spencer, a well-known balloonist, this craft flew from the Crystal Palace across London, but the journey appears to have been more windblown than controlled. In 1905 F. A. Barton built a larger craft; although it made some sort of flight, carrying the designer and four passengers, it was clearly also seriously underpowered. Neither craft could really be described as successful, and the true originator of non-rigid airships in this country was undoubtedly Ernest T. Willows, the son of a Cardiff dentist.

Willows' first craft was built in 1905, and in September that year it made what was probably the first controlled flight by a British airship, one that lasted for over an hour. The dirigible was small, however, being only 72 feet long and with a capacity of 12,000 cubic feet. It was inspected by Colonel J. E. Capper on behalf of the War Office, but although he was apparently impressed no governmental support was offered. Ernest Willows continued to develop his ideas, eventually becoming the first man to fly an airship across the English Channel from England to France. Unfortunately he was always hampered by lack of money and he never achieved the results of which he was almost certainly capable.

A year later Colonel Capper became head of the Army Balloon Factory at Farnborough and in 1907, aided by S. F. Cody, he built Britain's first military dirigible, the *Nulli Secundus*. It had a 50 hp Antoinette engine, a length of 122 feet, a capacity of 55,000 cubic feet and a top speed of about 16 mph. On 15th October, 1907, it flew nearly fifty miles from Aldershot to the Crystal Palace, but it was unable to make the return journey because of strong adverse winds and had to be deflated and brought back by road to the Balloon Factory. Rebuilt as a semi-rigid and enlarged the following year, it proved to be slightly faster at around 20 mph, but this was still inadequate for practical purposes. Shortly afterwards the airship was broken up.

That same year of 1908 saw a surprising development when the Committee of Imperial Defence decided to commission a large rigid airship, to be modelled on what could be learned about the design of the latest Zeppelins. Vickers, the shipbuilders of Barrow-in-Furness, had some experience of building submarines, and this was apparently considered sufficient qualification; their tender was accepted the following year and work soon began.

Meanwhile, the Royal Engineers of the Balloon Factory—soon to become the Royal Aircraft Establishment—had made another non-rigid airship, much smaller than *Nulli Secundus*, only 84 feet long and with a capacity of 21,000 cubic feet. Appropriately named *Baby*, it was also designated British Army Airship No 3, following the two variants of *Nulli Secundus* as No 1 and No 2. The envelope of this new dirigible was made of goldbeater's skin, a non-porous lightweight material derived from part of the outer membrane of the large intestine of cattle, the use of which had been pioneered by the balloonists of the Royal Engineers. The little ship first flew in May, 1909, and despite a top speed of only 20 mph showed promise. Accordingly, a year later it was rebuilt and renamed *Beta*. It was now longer, larger and faster, being 104 feet in length, with a capacity of 35,000 cubic feet, and capable of carrying a crew of three at some 25 mph for five hours. A further rebuilding, completed in 1912, made the craft

slightly larger and provided a much more powerful engine of 50 hp that gave a quite adequate top speed of 35 mph. This was the first really practicable military airship to be made and flown in Britain, and only the rather erratic Willows machines could possibly claim an earlier success.

Beta became well known to the British public over the next few years and was also a general favourite with all the servicemen who flew and trained in it. Among other incidents in its career it was used for bomb dropping trials, was fitted experimentally with a machine-gun, was inspected by King George V, and took the Prince of Wales for a half-hour flight. Its career extended into wartime, and before the war it became the first airship to be fitted with lightweight radio equipment specially designed by Captain H. P. Lefroy, of the Royal Engineers, an unsung benefactor of the airship service. On 27th January, 1911, *Beta* transmitted messages from the air back to Farnborough, although, due to the noise, reception was possible only when the engine was stopped for brief periods.

In 1910 a similar but slightly larger airship was constructed at the Army Balloon Factory and this became known as *Gamma*. Unlike *Beta*, its envelope was of rubberized fabric, a material used exclusively for non-rigid airships from then on. One notable feature of the design was the use of twin swivelling propellers, fitted as an aid to manoeuvring. Like its predecessor, *Gamma* was rebuilt and modified during its career and eventually reached a capacity of 101,000 cubic feet, which permitted a crew of six to be carried in addition to radio equipment—wireless telegraphy or W/T as it was then termed. During the 1912 Army manoeuvres the *Gamma*, captained by the enterprising Major Edward

Opposite page: The *Nulli Secundus* was designed and built in 1907 by Colonel Capper and Samuel F. Cody. On 5th October that year it was flown by its two inventors from Farnborough to central London, where it circled Trafalgar Square, Buckingham Palace and St Paul's. A strong headwind slowed the airship to a crawl on the return flight and it was forced to land at the Crystal Palace. After a vain wait for better weather the airshipmen deflated the envelope and returned everything to Farnborough by road. *Fleet Air Arm Museum*

Right: Major Edward Maitland, who began his career in the Essex Regiment, was an early enthusiast for the airship. He went on to serve with the Royal Naval Air Service and the RAF, eventually reaching the rank of Air Commodore.

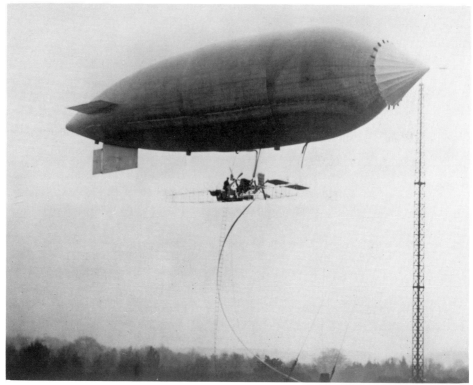

The *Beta* was involved in many pioneering experiments. She became the first non-rigid airship to be attached to a mooring mast when she took part in trials at Farnborough on 19th and 20th February, 1912, during which winds of up to 33 mph were recorded.   *Fleet Air Arm Museum*

Maitland, observed the attacking enemy and reported back so efficiently that the exercises ended in victory for the defending forces a day earlier than the time allowed.

The year that saw the appearance of *Beta* and *Gamma* also saw an embarrassing episode when two French airships were reluctantly purchased by the War Office, goaded by vociferous public opinion. The cost of the shed for the first, a Clement-Bayard dirigible, was largely covered by a subscription raised by the *Daily Mail* newspaper. On 16th October it flew from Compiègne to Wormwood Scrubs with a crew of seven, averaging 41 mph with the benefit of a following wind, and on the way became the first airship to cross the English Channel. Unfortunately this proved to be its sole achievement, for after the airship had been dismantled and transported by road to Farnborough the envelope was found to be in such poor condition that the entire airship had to be written off.

The second French dirigible was a Lebaudy paid for by subscribers of the *Morning Post* newspaper. It left Moisson for Farnborough only ten days after the Clement-Bayard, carrying a crew of six, including Major Sir Alex Bannerman. It reached Farnborough safely, but was damaged when being forced into the insufficiently high hangar. After the makers had repaired the ship and the War Department had raised the shed, the Lebaudy proved difficult to control; she finally wrapped herself around a house when returning from a trial flight.

In February, 1911, the Royal Engineers of the Army Balloon Factory were transformed into the Air Battalion, commanded by Sir Alex Bannerman. There were two companies, of which No 2 was concerned only with aeroplanes, while No 1, commanded by Major Maitland, dealt only with airships. This officer, formerly of the Essex Regiment, was a famous balloonist who in 1908 had flown all the way to Russia. He was a strong proponent of both the airship and the parachute, frequently taking considerable risks to prove the viability of one or the other.

Later in 1911, the ambitious rigid airship ordered in 1909 by the Committee of Imperial Defence for the Admiralty finally reached completion. She was of the mathematically determined "Zahm" shape, with parallel sides separating the rounded bow and tapering stern, and she strongly resembled contemporary

Naval Airship No 1 after the accident on 24th September, 1911, which ended her short career. Although the damage she sustained when leaving her shed at Barrow is usually ascribed to a powerful gust of wind, the true reason for the disaster would appear to have been inept handling by the inexperienced ground crew. *Fleet Air Arm Museum*

German designs. Known officially as Naval Rigid Airship No 1, she was unofficially named *Mayfly*, even before her disastrous ending. She was launched in May, and four months were then spent in modification and attempts to make her airworthy. However, she never flew. On 24th September, when she was being manoeuvred backwards out of her shed, someone apparently forgot to untether the lines at her bows. Despite being sturdily constructed of the new alloy duralumin, she was broken in two by the handling party and had to be ignominiously scrapped.

The next year, 1912, proved to be a crucial one in many ways. At the beginning of the year, following the disillusion of the *Mayfly* episode, the Admiralty closed down the special section set up to develop naval airships and discontinued all such experiments. The Royal Flying Corps, which replaced the Air Battalion in April, was divided into an Army Wing and a Naval Wing, and the latter was soon known unofficially as the Naval Air Service. Later in the year a small committee of officers travelled to Germany to investigate the development there of military aeronautics. Their subsequent report to the Committee of Imperial Defence was so alarming that by September not only was the Naval Airship Section re-established but measures to develop an airship fleet for Britain were agreed upon as a matter of urgency. The two Army airships *Beta* and *Gamma* were joined by a similar but slightly larger version, *Delta*, during the course of the year, and it proved to be equally successful. Twin swivelling propellers were again fitted, powered by two 105 hp engines, and these gave it a

A Lebaudy airship of the type acquired by the War Office in 1910. Paid for by subscribers of the *Morning Post*, this airship had a relatively short and unsuccessful career before being wrecked on the roof of a house. *Robert Malster*

The Astra Torres airship ordered from France became Naval Airship No 3. She is seen here moored to one of the experimental mooring masts with which trials were carried out at Farnborough. Her trilobe envelope made No 3 the technical ancestor of many wartime airships.

top speed in excess of 40 mph—no slower, it is worth noticing, than that of the Bristol Boxkite aeroplanes then being flown by the RFC. It was from *Delta* that a year later Edward Maitland made the world's first parachute descent from an airship, landing damp but unharmed in an Aldershot reservoir.

A final Army airship appeared in 1913, very much the same as its predecessors and known as *Eta*. (*Epsilon* was designed but never built; *Zeta* was to have been the Clement-Bayard). One pioneering feature was a new method of attaching the suspension wires to the envelope. The very first airships had used netting, as with balloons, but this had been largely superseded by a "rigging band" comprising a rope or canvas reinforcement of the envelope. The method used on *Eta* was to attach the rigging wires to steel D-rings, through which cotton or silk webbing pieces passed. These were sewn or stuck on the envelope with strengthening pieces of fabric, each assembly becoming known as an "Eta patch" thereafter.

The new airship, together with the others, was also fitted with a more advanced type of radio equipment by Captain Lefroy, and it was found that *Eta* and *Delta* could exchange messages even when a hundred miles apart: a significant development.

In the meantime, the Admiralty had hastily bought the only available civilian airship in this country, the Willows No 4, which now became Naval Airship No 2 and was destined for training purposes. An Astra Torres airship was ordered from France and—since Zeppelins were not for sale—a Parseval from Germany. The Astra Torres, built by a French firm but designed by a Spaniard, one Torres Quevedo, was of a very original design and one that was to have considerable influence on later British developments. She possessed a gasbag of a trefoil or "trilobe" section, with the three lobes connected internally and maintained in shape by porous fabric curtains. This method of construction produced greater stiffness than the conventional form and also allowed the rigging lines to be slung internally from the ridges on either side of the upper lobe, enabling their external length to be shorter and so reducing head resistance. At her official trials the Astra Torres reached a speed of 51.1 mph, a world record for airships.

The Parseval was large for a non-rigid, being of some 310,000 cubic feet capacity and with a length of 276 feet. The streamlining of her envelope was the most advanced of the time, giving her an exceptionally graceful appearance, although the suspension lines were rather long, to distribute the weight of a much shorter car than was usual. Two ballonets were fitted, at either end of the envelope, and these not only maintained internal pressure but could be operated separately to adjust the trim. Alternatively, this could be done by moving the car forward or aft by means of pulleys on the rigging. Elevators were not originally fitted, but these were added after the trial flights.

These two foreign non-rigids were eventually delivered and became Naval Airships No 3 and No 4 respectively. Plans to buy another Parseval and three Forlaninis from Italy were rendered abortive by the onset of war, while the planned building on licence of two more Parsevals was postponed for many months. However, in spite of the *Mayfly* fiasco, two more rigid airships were ordered from Vickers. There was also a tentative plan to order two rigids from Armstrong Whitworth, to be known as No 14 and No 15, but this plan was never implemented.

On 1st January, 1914, all the Army airships were handed over to the Navy, and those military airship personnel who, like Edward Maitland, did not trust aeroplanes were allowed to transfer. This division of interest was confirmed some months later on 1st July, 1914, when the Naval Wing of the RFC formally became the Royal Naval Air Service, a separate organization under the control of the Admiralty. The airship section, which became known as the Airship Service, comprised only 198 men of all ranks and was headed by Commander E. A. D. Masterman.

When the Great War broke out on 4th August, 1914, Britain's airship fleet consisted of the four former Army blimps (now known as Naval Airships Nos 17, 18, 19 and 20), the two foreigners and the small Willows training craft: seven in all. Of airfields possessing hangars capable of housing such unwieldy aircraft there were as yet only four, at Farnborough, at the Vickers yard in Barrow, at Wormwood Scrubs, and at Kingsnorth, near Hoo on the Medway.

CHAPTER FOUR

The First Operations

A T THE outbreak of war aeroplanes and airships were undeveloped and still largely experimental, and few of either their potentialities or their limitations were well understood, even by those best qualified to judge. The RNAS had at first only the vaguely defined role of acting in support of the Navy by providing a reconnaissance force, but exactly how this was to be done was at first a matter for debate and experiment.

The very first air action of the war was carried out within twenty-four hours of the declaration of hostilities by the crew of a naval aircraft with perhaps a greater appreciation of their own enterprise than of their exact role in the defence of Britain. On the evening of 5th August at 7 pm Naval Airship No 4, the German-built Parseval, lifted off from Kingsnorth carrying a crew of five captained by Lieutenant J. N. Fletcher, and flew out over the Thames estuary to seek any German warships that might be approaching.

Not long after the airship left, a distant flash in the sky was seen from Kingsnorth. This was due to lightning striking a small ammunition dump at Faversham, but was suspected to be the airship exploding. A message was immediately radioed asking her to acknowledge, but Lieutenant Fletcher decided not to do so, since he had express orders to break radio silence only in the event of enemy activity. Some time afterwards the crew of the airship came upon a group of British minesweepers in an area where no friendly ships were expected and assumed them to be German minelayers or invaders. Wary of being shot at in the bright moonlight, Lieutenant Fletcher hastily increased height and distanced the airship from the flotilla, at the same time reporting the matter to base. Fortunately for everyone, the W/T operators at Kingsnorth had been confirmed in their fears by the lack of a response to their earlier message and so were no longer listening in. The airship's signals went unheard and no tragic consequences resulted from the mistaken identification.

After daybreak, flying home at a low height near the Kentish shore, the airship was hoist with her own petard and fired upon by soldiers of an encamped Territorial Division who believed her—not entirely without reason, despite the large White Ensign she carried—to be a raiding German aircraft. No damage was sustained, however, and P.4, as she was usually called, arrived back home safely if unexpectedly at 5.30 am after a patrol of ten and a half hours. For several days afterwards, it is said, the authorities were plagued by numerous reports from people claiming to have seen a marauding Zeppelin.

During the next few weeks the British Expeditionary Force was ferried across the Channel to Calais, so No 3 and No 4 carried out constant patrols to guard against enemy attacks on the troopships. Both airships flew from Kingsnorth, but as No 4 required refuelling more frequently than No 3, the Astra Torres, the former kept to the Straits of Dover while the latter flew further to the north-east to guard the approaches. Even when the Expeditionary Force was safely in France the patrolling continued, although less intensively.

Later in the same month a small number of RNAS aeroplanes and armoured cars was sent across to Ostend to support a detachment of British troops and marines preparing to defend the city. Accompanying the force was No 3, captained by Wing Commander N. F. Usborne, which was moored out in the open without sustaining harm for three days, until the entire operation was abandoned and everyone was evacuated to Dunkirk. Before returning to Britain No 3 flew boldly over Ostend in daylight to find out whether or not the Germans had yet entered the city.

Back in England, No 3 joined *Beta* and *Eta* in making night-time flights over London in an attempt to check the lighting and to evaluate the difficulties that would be experienced by attacking Zeppelins. On the evening of 22nd September, which was both dark and foggy, *Beta* flew from Wormwood Scrubs, but although keeping to a height of only about 500 feet she soon became lost. Eventually the crew recognized Golders Green underground station by its name picked out in electric lights, and after coming down even lower, to around 300 feet, the airship was able to follow the main roads and thus to regain her base. Four nights later No 3 also flew for an hour over London to provide practice for the searchlight crews.

Shortly afterwards another RNAS party, this time under the command of Wing Commander Maitland, was sent out to Firminy, near Dunkirk, to establish a balloon base in a disused factory. They took some spherical balloons with them, and *Eta* set out to join the group. Unhappily, on her way she was obliged to make a forced landing at Redhill and was badly damaged, so *Beta* flew out as a replacement and was soon carrying out reconnaissance work as well as artillery control for the Belgian guns nearby. The balloons, intended to help monitors lying offshore with gun control, proved to be markedly inferior in any sort of wind to the sausage-shaped Drachen kite balloons used by the Belgians and modelled on German practice. Maitland was allowed to inspect, photograph and measure these balloons, and before long Britain also was using aircraft frankly copied from the enemy's designs—not for the last time.

Very soon the party was recalled. Although kite balloons had an obvious role and were soon being built in considerable numbers, the best use to which airships could be put remained uncertain. It had at least become clear, however, following the recent combat experiences, that both *Beta* and No 3 had been lucky to survive. Defended only with rifles or revolvers and operating on the enemy's doorstep, they would have fallen easy prey to any armed aeroplanes they might have encountered, since these could certainly have out-manoeuvred them. The comparatively large bulk of the airships, moreover, combined with their slow speed and the low altitudes at which they were obliged to fly, made them potentially easy targets for high angle guns. But while junior officers discussed the shortcomings of their craft and wondered at their future role, the question was resolved for them by the enemy and by the march of events.

The loss of Zeebrugge, Ostend and the Belgian coastline to the Germans had altered the strategic situation and allowed the enemy to make full use of what could well have been the decisive weapon of the war. Just as the influence of aircraft on future conflicts had been almost totally unappreciated before 1914, so also had the terrifying potential of the torpedo-firing submarine. Britain needed to import great quantities of food and raw materials in order to live and carry on fighting, and all of this had to come by sea. Once the stalemate of trench warfare took over on land, the Germans attempted to destroy Britain, their principal enemy, by cutting off that seaborne trade on which she depended so absolutely. Never before used in any major conflict, these submarine or U-boats (*Unterseebooten*) were almost invincible in their invisibility.

Sailing from the newly acquired bases on the Belgian coast, the U-boats

Beta flew by night over London during the early days of the war to evaluate the difficulties that might be faced by attacking Zeppelins. The hazards of navigating by night were revealed when her crew became lost on 22nd September, 1914.   *Imperial War Museum*

found their slow speed of about 10 knots on the surface or 7 knots submerged only a minor handicap, and they began to sink British shipping with impunity, at first only warships but soon merchantmen and passenger liners as well. The menace of the submarine quickly became the single most important factor of the war and far more threatening to the nation's wellbeing than the Zeppelin raids which were soon arousing so much terror and hatred in the general public. During the first few months of the war attacks on British warships had occurred only near Scapa Flow in the Orkneys or along the Scottish east coast, but in 1915 the marauding submarines moved southwards into the English Channel and the Irish Sea. Attempts by British seaplanes flying from Dunkirk or Dover to block the Straits were in vain, and bombing raids on the submarines' bases proved equally ineffective.

On 23rd November the ss *Malachite* was shelled off Le Havre for half an hour by a submarine, and on New Year's Day the battleship HMS *Formidable* was sunk near the Isle of Wight with the loss of 547 lives. At the end of the same month the submarine *U.21*, which had sunk the light cruiser HMS *Pathfinder* off the Firth of Forth in September, actually surfaced with remarkable prescience off Barrow-in-Furness and fired several shells at the Vickers airship shed, fortunately without causing much damage. There were other such incidents, and on 4th February the German Admiralty announced that all the waters around Great Britain would be regarded from the 18th onwards as a war zone in which all British ships would be sunk and all neutral vessels must proceed at their own risk.

In Britain the First Sea Lord, Lord Fisher, realized that the situation was critical and that rapid short-term measures must be taken, if necessary at the expense of more long-term projects. The First Lord of the Admiralty, Winston Churchill, had recently cancelled the order for the two large rigid airships which Vickers had been planning since 1913 and on one of which work had already started, but Lord Fisher still believed that airships, albeit of a different type, could provide part of the answer he was seeking.

On 28th February he called a meeting at the Admiralty, which was attended by Commander Masterman, senior RNAS officers and representatives of two firms: Airships Ltd and Armstrong Whitworth Ltd. They were told that a new type of airship was urgently required, for which the basic requirements were a speed of between 40 and 50 mph and the ability to carry a crew of two, 160 lb of bombs, W/T equipment and fuel for eight hours' flying. They should be able to reach an altitude of 5,000 feet and their design had to be simple, in order both to ease production and to facilitate the training of aircrew.

Most importantly, the first of the new airships—to be designated SS, for Submarine Scout—had to be in the air within weeks rather than months. The two firms were invited to tender, and the RNAS were also asked to prepare their own design.

CHAPTER FIVE

The Early SS Airships

HOLT THOMAS, the head of Airships Ltd, and his designer Ernest Willows raced to build an airship that would satisfy the Admiralty's requirements. The craft they produced became known as SS.2; she was delivered to Kingsnorth for evaluation tests towards the end of March.

She was of 70,000 cubic feet capacity, 140 feet in length and had a rather elaborate car which was lengthened by spars at both ends to distribute its weight more evenly on the envelope, to which it was attached by a novel system of wooden toggles. The engine was a 100 hp Curtiss; it drove two swivelling propellers in a manner which Willows had already used in earlier dirigibles and which he believed was essential to good control. Although undoubtedly efficient, this transmission feature employed three gearboxes and so was expensive to produce and required skill to operate. On both counts the specification requirements had been ignored, but Willows refused to compromise when he was asked to provide a simpler and cheaper arrangement. The envelope of SS.2, made from doped instead of rubberized fabric, also proved unsatisfactory and was another factor in deciding the Admiralty not to proceed further with the Willows design. SS.2 herself was very soon scrapped.

The firm of Armstrong Whitworth eventually also produced a prototype design which became known as SS.27, and they later received further orders. However, it was the men of the RNAS themselves who produced the ideal craft for their service. Apparently there had already been informal discussion among the officers involved, and a meeting was held in the mess at Farnborough on the very same evening that Admiral Fisher made his needs known. Those involved were Wing Commander N. F. Usborne, the CO at Kingsnorth, Flight Lieutenant Cave-Browne-Cave and F. M. Green of the Royal Aircraft Factory. Fully aware of the urgency of the problem, they came up with a solution both simple and effective which made use of already existing material. The spare 35,000-cubic-feet envelope of No 2, the small Willows training ship, which had been stored at Farnborough, was at once appropriated, together with its valves, planes and rigging, and taken to Kingsnorth, which had been designated as a constructional and experimental station. An old fuselage from a B.E.2c aeroplane was also acquired and was attached to the envelope by means of Eta patches and altered rigging. A 70 hp Renault engine was fitted, and a small auxiliary blower forced air into the two ballonets as required.

During the first trial flight the elevators were found to be overbalanced and

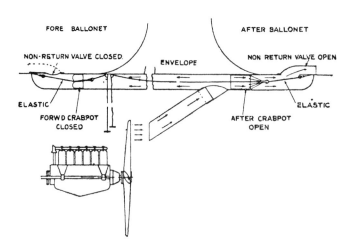

Left: A schematic drawing of the blower pipe and valves of a non-rigid airship such as an SS ship.

Opposite page: One of the earliest SS airships, fitted with two lower vertical planes and rudders in order to increase manoeuvrability. The original B.E.2c undercarriage has been retained.
Imperial War Museum

the nose was driven in by air pressure at speed. These were minor problems; the elevators were quickly modified and the nose strengthened by stiff canes positioned radially. At the same time, the internal pressure of the envelope was increased by removing the air blower and fixing behind the propeller a metal scoop, which was thus fed by the full force of the slipstream. This air was fed by a tube into the after ballonet; the forward ballonet was removed. A vertical wheel was fixed in the cockpit to operate the elevators, and the usual aeroplane foot steering bar was retained for rudder control.

These modifications provided to be very effective and on 18th March, after Lieutenant W. Hicks had conducted the final trials and less than three weeks after work had begun, the new airship was commissioned as SS.1 and entered service. Admiral Fisher expressed his approval with a curt "Now I must have forty!"

Within days work was contracted out to various firms, and copies of the new airship were soon being produced. The most difficult problem was ensuring the supply of envelopes, as the usual manufacturers were too busy with aeroplane orders to accept any new work. The answer was provided by Wing Commander Usborne, who personally visited six firms specializing in waterproof clothing or rubber goods, placed the orders directly and arranged for representatives to visit Kingsnorth to learn how to prepare the material correctly.

The production SS airships differed somewhat from the prototype, mainly in having a larger envelope and two ballonets. As time went on other variants appeared, all basically similar but differing in details. Apart from SS.2 already mentioned, and SS.3 which was built by Short Bros to the same general pattern, all the airships up to SS.26 were based on SS.1. The Airship Company produced a car based on the Maurice Farman aeroplane fuselage and this was used for airships SS.28 to SS.39, with the temporary exception of SS.34, which flew for a

while with the car from *Beta*. A third type of car belatedly produced by Armstrong Whitworth was also based on a normal aeroplane fuselage. This was tried out on SS.27 and, having been found to provide a greater endurance than the other versions, was used from SS.39A to SS.47. The last two airships of this class, SS.48 and SS.49, were both sold to France and used the original B.E.2c type car.

The B.E.2c type had an envelope with a capacity of 60,000 cubic feet, which was 143 feet in length and had a maximum diameter of 28 feet. The nose was stiffened by twenty-four radially positioned canes held at the centre by a small aluminium conical cap and covered with fabric. There were two interconnected ballonets, each with a capacity of 6,375 cubic feet and each equipped with an automatic valve set to open at a lower pressure than a similar valve at the bottom of the gasbag proper. The air to the ballonets was ducted from the slipstream and controlled by two "crab pot" valves, operated by cords. As well as maintaining internal pressure by compensating for loss of gas, these enabled the trim to be altered; admitting air only to the forward ballonet caused the nose to drop, while admitting it only to the rear ballonet had the opposite effect. There was also a spring-loaded valve on top of the envelope from which an operating cord led through a special leakproof gland packed with grease down into the car, while another cord provided a method of ensuring closure. The automatic gas and air valves on the underside of the envelope were also fitted with cords ending in toggles and so could be operated manually if necessary. At the rear of the envelope were positioned radially two horizontal planes incorporating the elevators and braced by wires leading to Eta patches. Beneath these was a lower vertical plane, or sometimes two set at a slight angle to each other. The latter arrangement, which provided two rudders, was usually preferred since it gave greater control, but the former was often chosen in order to obtain a rather

One of the earliest SS airships, probably SS.16, with a B.E.2c type of car which retains the original wheeled undercarriage. The engine is a 75 hp Renault driving a nine-foot four-bladed propeller.
Fleet Air Arm Museum

The Maurice Farman car, seen here on an SS airship operating from Pulham, was shorter than the B.E.2c type and had the advantage that the pusher layout saved the crew from buffeting by the slipstream. In the background the Pulham No 2 shed and windscreen can be seen in course of erection. *Royal Aeronautical Society*

The cockpit and controls of an SS airship with B.E.2c car. According to the Admiralty Handbook on SS Type Airships "the arrangement of valve and crab-pot cords varies to some extent according to the taste of individual pilots", but this shows the usual arrangement.

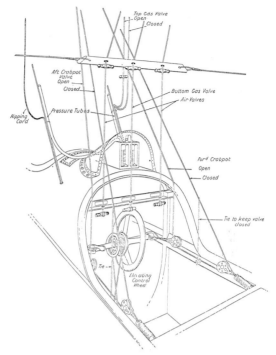

higher top speed. In this case, the single rudder was increased in area. Six handling guys were provided, and a trail rope, 120 feet long, could be used with or without a grapnel.

The car on the first models retained its normal aeroplane undercarriage of wheels, but these were sometimes replaced with floats on later versions or even discarded entirely. Eight 16 lb bombs were carried on a rack beneath the car and two 65 lb bombs were placed below the pilot's seat. Above the engine was a petrol tank with an external gauge. This fed by gravity to the engine and was replenished from the intermediate tank placed in the fuselage and the bottom tank below the front seat. Fuel was forced up by air pressure provided by operating a hand pump fixed outside the car on the port side. Altogether, the three tanks held about 60 gallons. A small tank behind the engine held three gallons of oil, and a canvas ballast bag containing 14 gallons of water was positioned behind the pilot, who was accompanied only by a W/T operator in the front cockpit. His radio was powered by accumulators, since no generator was provided, and he could receive and transmit up to 80 miles in suitable conditions. The aerial was unwound from a reel and hung down about 200 feet, prevented by a lead weight from fouling any part of the airship. An emergency aerial, to be used when the airship was close to the ground, was formed by two wires extending back to the horizontal tail planes.

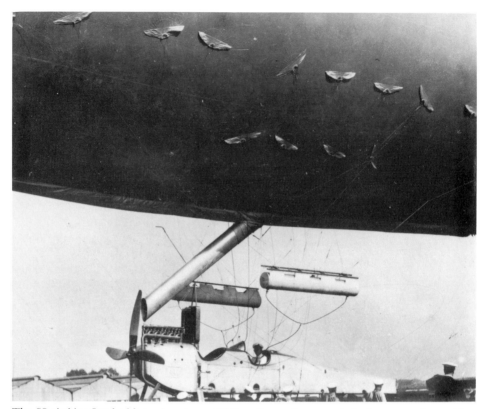

The SS airships fitted with an Armstrong Whitworth car always used the larger envelope with a 70,000 cubic feet capacity. The petrol was in two tanks suspended below the envelope. The Eta patches by which the rigging lines were attached to the envelope can be clearly seen in this photograph.   *Fleet Air Arm Museum*

Both cockpits were protected from the slipstream only by small triplex windshields, and in the rear one was positioned a dashboard fitted with various instruments. These usually included a rev. counter, an inclinometer, an altimeter, an airspeed indicator, a statoscope—to indicate rise or fall—and a manometer, which registered the gas pressure. At night the instruments were illuminated from batteries or accumulators. Directly in front of the pilot was positioned a liquid-filled magnetic compass, and there was also a clock, which he had to remember to wind up regularly. The engine was usually an eight-cylinder air-cooled 75 hp Renault driving a four-bladed propeller through a reduction gear of 2 to 1 and with a maximum safety limit of 1,800 revolutions per minute. Like most aero-engines of the time it was rather unreliable; anyone carrying out repairs in mid-air had to balance precariously on the skids, holding on with one hand and working with the other. Then he had to start the engine by swinging the propeller!

The Maurice Farman variants differed somewhat from their predecessors, principally in employing a pusher propeller and in sometimes having an enlarged envelope of 70,000 cubic feet capacity. A single fuel tank was fitted containing up to 64 gallons; this was immediately in front of the engine, to which it fed by gravity. A tube passed through the tank, so enabling an engine starting handle to be used. The water ballast was contained in a metal tank below the seats, while the oil was kept in three small cylinders, to be used in turn. Unlike the other two types of SS ship, the pilot normally sat in the front cockpit, although the controls were duplicated so that the airship could be handled in emergencies from the rear seat. However, this extra provision was frequently dispensed with in order to save unnecessary weight.

The Armstrong Whitworth type of SS ship always used the enlarged, 70,000 cubic feet envelope, as this was necessary to cope with the increased weight of the six-cylinder water-cooled 100 hp Green engine that was fitted. Several minor improvements over the earlier ships were made, although the bomb load was slightly reduced. The engine could be started by hand from the front seat and fuel was now gravity fed from two aluminium tanks hanging down from each side of the envelope and holding a total of 90 gallons. The same arrangement

SS.13 was renumbered SS.14A by the commanding officer at Pulham after a minor accident on 13th October, 1917. A month later, on the same station, C.13 became C.14A. At the time of the Armistice SS.14A was the oldest of all airships remaining in active service. *Fleet Air Arm Museum*

was sometimes fitted retrospectively to some Maurice Farman type ships when later modifications to improve the engine's performance required a more effective fuel feed.

Most of the SS ships could reach a speed of about 50 mph, although the Maurice Farman types were rather slower, and all could remain aloft for at least ten hours. They seldom flew at a height of more than 4,000 feet, climbing usually at around 700 feet a minute, but SS.5 once climbed to 10,000 feet in 25 minutes and SS.23 was reputed to have dived safely from 1,100 feet to 100 feet in 56 seconds. The time taken to turn a complete circle varied, but was normally well under a minute.

Ten badly damaged SS airships were either replaced or extensively repaired, and in these cases the same number was re-issued, but with a suffix. If these ten are all regarded as new rather than renovated, then fifty-nine SS airships were built for the Admiralty altogether, of which ten were sold to Italy and four to France. Of those retained in British service, nine were either wrecked in some way or lost at sea and twenty-seven were deleted before the end of the war as no longer serviceable. There are oddities in the list (see Appendix), such as SS.10, which was rebuilt once as SS.10A, then rebuilt a second time as SS.10B before being sold to Italy. And it was surely only superstition which dictated that after SS.13 had been in a minor accident on the 13th of the month she should be redesignated SS.14A without being considered a new aircraft. Ironically, perhaps, she became one of only nine SS ships still active on 11th November, 1918, and also the longest-serving wartime airship of any class.

Probably the only British airship ever to fly over enemy territory, SS.40 was fitted with a larger envelope and painted with black dope for service in France. She was the only airship to be used during wartime by the British Army, and her observer was consequently the only English soldier to see active service in a dirigible.   *Fleet Air Arm Museum*

Few of these small blimps performed any great deeds, but manned by crews hastily recruited from the battleships at Scapa Flow and quickly trained on the airships already in service they soon proved their worth, watching, guarding and protecting Allied shipping. Sadly, the airship which had provided the pattern for this work, SS.1, was the first to be deleted. On 7th May, 1915, less than two months after being accepted, she was flying into Capel at 8.40 pm when the pilot, Sub-Lieutenant R. Booth, mistook the wind signal and tried to land downwind. The airship was swept into some telegraph wires and crashed in flames, the two occupants falling clear and escaping without serious injury.

In the Dardanelles campaign of 1915 and 1916 a small group of SS ships—known as the Airship Expeditionary Force—was active in anti-submarine patrols, convoy duty and photographic reconnaissance. These craft were also very successful in detecting mines, while SS.7 even carried out artillery spotting for HMS *Venerable* and HMS *Talbot* on the night of 25th–26th September, 1915. She flew close to the shore at an altitude of 3,800 feet, but despite bright moonlight her crew were unable to see the targets clearly enough to give significant help. Nevertheless, the small airships were clearly viewed as a threat by the enemy since they had to be protected by seaplanes from attack; one hostile aeroplane even attempted to drop a bomb directly on top of a cruising blimp. However, no airships were lost, despite long patrols which involved their crews' spending many hours cramped into the narrow cockpits. SS.3, SS.7, SS.8, SS.17 and SS.19 were all involved in the Mediterranean and all survived until deleted on the same day in April, 1918. Before then they had been joined by SS.40, an airship with a most unusual history.

She was in fact the only airship ever to go on active service with the British army, for in 1916 she was loaned to the British Expeditionary Force for experimental use over the Western Front. It was thought by some senior officers that a small airship would be ideal both for night reconnaissance and for putting down agents behind the enemy lines. Accordingly, the RFC sent a representative to Polegate, where SS.40's envelope was painted with black dope and her engine made quieter. A trial was held in cloudless conditions on the night of 30th/31st May, 1916, when it was found that up to a height of about 4,000 feet the airship could be both seen and heard, but at 5,000 feet or above she became invisible and could not be located even by searchlights. When the engine was throttled back she was also quite inaudible.

These results appeared encouraging, so the airship was flown to France on 6th July in the charge of Sub-Lieutenant W. P. C. Chambers. She did not arrive at her specially built canvas-covered shed at Frévent until the next day, however, having spent the intervening night at Marquise due to engine trouble. The Navy had sent out riggers, W/T operators and an engineer, but the Army had provided a ground crew of forty soldiers, under the command of a single officer. On the 19th the airship had to return to Polegate to change her envelope for a larger one, since the original would now not lift her above 3,000 feet, presumably because of the extra weight of operational equipment.

She came back to France the very next day as the new envelope was not ready, and spent three days in various forms of practice before returning to England on the 24th, when the new envelope was ready to be fitted. Two days later she was back once more in France, only for her pilot to find that the new envelope still gave an insufficient margin of lift. There was more practice, including the dropping of a dummy by parachute, and on 8th August she returned yet again to Polegate for a third envelope, this time of 83,000 cubic feet capacity. Within two days she was flying again from Frévent and in practice reached an altitude of 8,000 feet, much higher than was considered necessary.

On the night of 28th/29th August, SS.40 left Frévent at 11 pm and for the first time flew across the lines near Arras, carrying an Army observer, and returning safely two and a half hours later. Low clouds, bright moonlight, bad weather and further engine troubles all limited flying during the next three weeks, but on 26th September, piloted by Sub-Lieutenant Chambers and carrying 2nd Lieutenant C. R. Robbins of the RFC and RFA as the observer, she again crossed the lines. This time the flight lasted three hours and the airship ventured as far as Cambrai before returning home and crossing the lines at Loos. Many lights were seen, but most of the small towns and villages could be identified only tentatively; nothing of real interest or strategic importance was observed, except one or two trains.

Regrettably, this second flight over enemy territory confirmed suspicions that the airship was not really suitable for the task of night-time reconnaissance

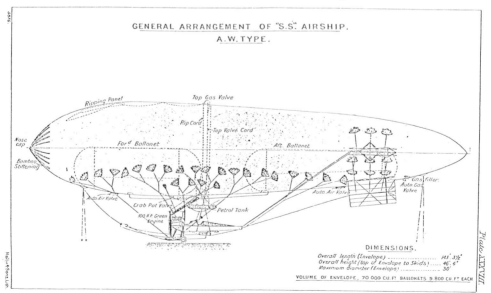

GENERAL ARRANGEMENT OF "S.S." AIRSHIP.
A.W. TYPE.

DIMENSIONS.

Overall length (Envelope) .... 143' 3½'
Overall height (top of Envelope to Skids) ..... 46' 4"
Maximum diameter (Envelope) .... 30'

VOLUME OF ENVELOPE, 70,000 CU. FT. BALLONETS 9,800 CU. FT. EACH

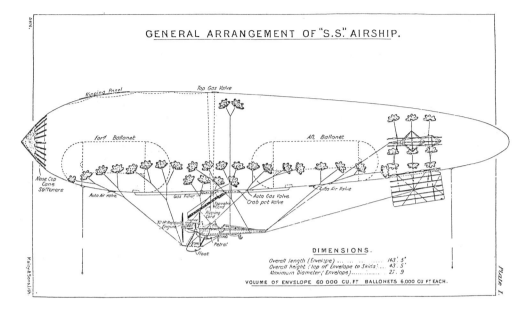

General arrangement drawings of the three main types of SS airship. Above is the original type with the B.E.2c car and below is the Maurice Farman type, both having envelopes with a capacity of 60,000 cubic feet. On the opposite page is the Armstrong Whitworth type with a 70,000 cubic feet capacity envelope.

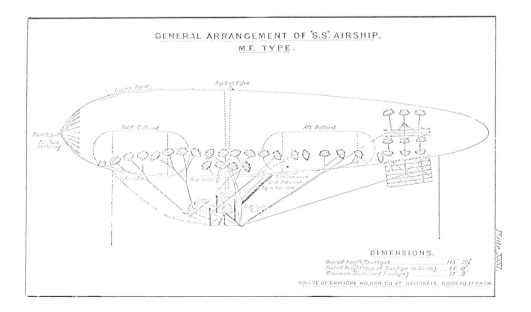

over land. She was too vulnerable to be risked in conditions of good visibility, while on those nights when darkness rendered her safe it was very difficult for her crew either to observe or to navigate properly. Her slow speed made any return flight against the prevailing westerly winds a further source of worry.

Despite this disappointment it was still believed that the dropping of agents might be carried out efficiently, so the Admiralty was asked to provide a new airship, equipped with a car specially adapted for the release of a parachutist. She was to be capable of flying at great heights and to have an envelope divided into separate compartments so that a few holes caused by rifle fire would not lead to a complete loss of gas. Nothing came of this proposal, though, for the RFC had by then experimented with parachute drops from aeroplanes and had concluded that no airship was required. Long before this, on 22nd September, 1916, SS.40 had returned to England and resumed normal duties. She was transferred to the Mediterranean soon afterwards and carried out useful if undramatic work there until scrapped as no longer serviceable at Kassandra on 1st October, 1918.

The careers of most SS ships were quietly efficient, and few were involved in dramatic incidents. Nevertheless, there were high points of tragedy, distinction and even humour. SS.39, an unlucky ship which was involved in more than one accident, killed Wing Commander C. M. Waterlow when he failed to release a handling guy and was lifted high into the air before falling to his death. By an unpleasant coincidence, his batman was later killed in a similar manner. SS.29 had the responsible but unpublicized task of escorting King George's ship both ways when he crossed the Channel to visit the troops in July, 1917.

SS.27 and SS.44 were both involved in somewhat bizarre incidents; the former hit a French church spire, while the latter went out of control, threw out one crew member and took the other to a great height hanging head downwards from the car. The ship eventually came down safely and both men escaped serious injury.

Flight Lieutenant E. F. Monk, the pilot of SS.42, suffered a very similar experience when the airship left Pembroke on 15th September, 1916, to look for a submarine that had been reported near Lundy Island. Bad weather compelled a return within two hours, but in attempting to land the airship was slammed into the ground by a strong gust of wind, snapping the trail rope and removing the port side suspensions, so causing the car to twist nearly upside down and throw out the W/T operator. The airship then soared into the air with petrol pouring out of the ruptured fuel tanks as the pilot clung on desperately, unable to operate any controls.

After some time, and at a height of around 7,000 feet, the forward suspensions also gave way and the car hung nose downwards, held only by the rear rigging. The pilot managed to keep hold and scramble to the undercarriage axle, where he perched precariously as the airship rose even higher through thick clouds, probably to about 8,500 feet. Eventually, some three hours after leaving Pembroke and having covered around a hundred miles, the airship began to fall, slowly at first but then faster, spinning as she did so. Just before she struck the ground near Ivybridge in Devon, Flight Lieutenant Monk jumped clear, landing heavily but escaping serious injury. The wreckage of the blimp was rebuilt as SS.42A, but she proved to be even less lucky in her second incarnation. Nearly a year later, with a different pilot, she was again damaged and drifted out to sea before coming down. By the time rescue ships appeared both members of the crew had drowned.

Despite such occasional tragedies as this, the first SS ships proved invaluable. They cost only some £2,500 each, and the proof of their usefulness is that production ceased only when something better became available.

One unfortunate derivative of the SS airships was the hybrid "airship-plane" designed by Squadron Commander W. P. Ireland and Wing Commander Usborne in an attempt to counter the Zeppelin threat. This was a complete B.E.2c aeroplane slung beneath an SS envelope. It was intended that the

This SS airship differs from that shown on page 25 in having a single vertical fin and rudder, fitted in order to obtain a slight increase in speed. Behind her can be seen a camouflaged windbreak intended to protect airships from gusts.   *Royal Aeronautical Society*

composite aircraft should at first handle like an airship—virtually a blimp with wings on the car—and so climb swiftly to the height at which Zeppelins operated. The composite would then split, the aeroplane going into action and the envelope—its valve having been opened—falling back to earth.

At the first trial in August, 1915, the device, piloted by Lieutenant Hicks, showed some promise, but due to faults appearing in the apparatus the units were not separated. Six months later the necessary modifications were completed and on 21st February, 1916, the AP.1, as it was designated, lifted off from Kingsnorth for a full trial carrying its two inventors as the crew. At about 4,000 feet matters went terribly wrong as the front suspensions were released prematurely, probably due to lack of pressure in the envelope. The weight of the engine tipped the aeroplane's nose forward, so straining and breaking the rear suspensions. The B.E.2c fell away, probably with its controls damaged, and at once side-slipped and turned over. Commander Ireland was thrown out and fell to his death in the Medway, while Commander Usborne, strapped in his seat, was killed as the aeroplane crashed into a goods yard. The Admiralty immediately banned any further experiments and AP.2, although already planned, never flew.

An unidentified SS airship of the Maurice Farman type taking part in mooring trials at sea. Such trials were carried out in the Wash by airships from Pulham, which served as an experimental station. A non-standard auxiliary blower appears to have been fitted to this airship to supply air to the ballonets while the engine is shut down.   *Fleet Air Arm Museum*

CHAPTER SIX

Strategy, Tactics and Policy

A S SOON as the SS airship programme was rushed into being in early 1915 the work of construction was transferred from Farnborough to Kingsnorth, which was soon joined as a manufacturing centre by Barrow and Wormwood Scrubs. At the same time new air stations were set up at Capel near Folkestone, Polegate near Eastbourne, Marquise near Boulogne on the French coast, Luce Bay near Stranraer, and in Anglesey. A new training station was set up at Cranwell.

In May Winston Churchill resigned as First Lord of the Admiralty and was succeeded by Arthur Balfour. Admiral Lord Fisher also left his post as First Sea Lord and was replaced by Sir Henry Jackson. There followed considerable reorganization and rationalization of the RNAS, with certain of its responsibilities, such as armoured cars and land-based balloons, being handed over to the Army, and the airship station at Marquise being passed back to the French.

More importantly, a rigid airship programme was inaugurated and work on the Vickers dirigible, which had been stopped earlier that year, was resumed. A new and larger class of non-rigids, the Coastal or C class, was also ordered. More air stations were planned, at Longside near Aberdeen, East Fortune on the Firth of Forth, Howden on the Humber, Pulham in Norfolk, Mullion in Cornwall and Pembroke in South Wales. Together with those already commissioned, they were soon providing a chain of bases strung round the coasts, from which airship patrols flew out regularly to combat submarines.

Under the energetic direction of Brigadier-General Masterman, hangars soon appeared, aircrews were recruited and trained, and all other necessary measures taken. Each station was placed under the control of the senior naval officer of the area, and co-operation between air and sea became of prime importance. Directional wireless stations were set up at strategic points, some of which only received and others of which could also transmit. Patrolling airships were required to transmit their call sign every hour, enabling their position to be found by cross bearings and their course to be plotted. An airship commander could then be informed of his exact location and so call for help to the precise spot: a vital element in the anti-submarine strategy envisaged by the Admiralty.

This was based essentially upon the fact that although no airship could ever carry more than a tiny fraction of the armament available to a destroyer or even an armed merchantman, yet no surface ship could approach the speed of an airship or command the same wide vision. The prime function of the airship, therefore, was to find the submarine and call for assistance, her own contribution to the actual attack being relatively unimportant.

In the event, matters were even simpler and the great virtue of the airships proved to be their deterrent value, which was outstanding, if unspectacular. From their bases all round the British coastline the little blimps patrolled the seas, watching constantly for any signs of the submarine enemy. They also looked for mines, which were then destroyed directly by gunfire or reported to minesweepers. Any wreckage which might endanger shipping or any vessels in distress were reported and—if necessary— guarded until help arrived. But it was the war against the U-boats which took priority.

In the clear waters of the Mediterranean a submerged enemy could often be discerned as deep as twelve fathoms or more, but in northern waters direct

The enemy! A German U-boat on the surface.   *Robert Malster*

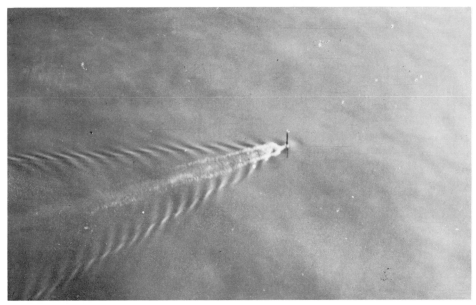

When submerged a submarine is invisible from the air in such waters as those of the North Sea, but under certain conditions the periscope leaves a visible and recognisable wake, known as a "feather".

Fleet Air Arm Museum

detection was more difficult, and in muddy estuaries quite impossible. Nonetheless, a periscope moving through the water made a distinctive "feather" of foamy wake and there were often other signs to give away the presence of a submarine. Small amounts of oil frequently leaked from propeller, rudder or hydroplane bearings, while larger amounts could appear if the submarine had sustained minor damage. In the Irish Sea it was common for seagulls to be attracted to the feather of the periscope, although oddly enough those in the North Sea appeared to ignore such an intrusion. On occasion the wake made by a torpedo in the water remained distinct for some time, enabling an airship to track it back to its source.

It soon became evident, also, that a submarine which had once attacked could very often not resist the temptation to remain in the area to find out whether it had been successful. More than once, by staying on watch for several hours, an airship was able to surprise a U-boat as it returned to the scene of its action.

Above all, a submarine commander could never be certain that he had evaded detection and in consequence he was obliged to proceed with caution, even when this was not really necessary. Submarines could recharge their batteries only when on the surface, so if forced to remain submerged their range and speed were both greatly reduced. These twin handicaps, forced upon them by the presence of airships, made it far more difficult for them to chase and outmanoeuvre warships or merchantmen. And at the same time, while still open to detection and attack from the airship the submarine was quite unable to fight back. To do this meant ascending to the surface in order to fire at the blimp, but any such action made the submarine not only immediately vulnerable to any warship but also to the airship herself if the shots missed. No submarine, in fact, seems to have taken this risk until towards the end of the war, and even then such retaliation was attempted only when no other vessel was in the vicinity; it was apparently never successful. With the possible exception of C.25, no airship was shot down by a submarine; the only blimps that were lost due to enemy action seem to have been the two destroyed near the Straits of Dover by aeroplanes operating towards the limit of their range. Even there the airships were able to keep an almost permanent vigil over the ships that crossed regularly to and from Calais; no troopship was ever torpedoed or sunk while escorted in this way.

The threat posed to the U-boats by the British airships was matched by a corresponding threat to the airships from the German aeroplanes, but with the crucial difference that the airships could nearly always reach the submarines, while the aeroplanes were rarely able to reach the airships. The German submarines had a limited range and were unable to venture far out into the Atlantic, so in order to intercept shipping bound for Liverpool, Bristol, Southampton or London they were obliged to operate in the Western Approaches to the English Channel. Here, as in most of the North Sea, they were within range of the British airships but too far from German-occupied territory for their own aeroplanes to intervene.

Most of the non-rigid airships operated under extreme handicaps, with their crews confined for many hours at a time to cold and windswept cockpits, having to cope with noisy, temperamental engines and without the possibility of sleep or rest. It was to overcome these problems that the North Sea class of non-rigids and the later rigid airships were planned, so that not only could these aircraft patrol further out, for longer periods and with greater reliability, but it would be possible for two crews to be carried, to eat and sleep on board, and to alternate spells of duty. Such airships came along too late to exert an appreciable influence on the war, however, and it is to the small blimps that the credit of defeating the submarine belongs.

During the first eighteen months of the war, up to the end of 1915, the Allies lost 568 ships. There was a lull towards the end of the year, due partly to a reluctance by the Germans to provoke America and partly to the need to transfer their U-boats to the Mediterranean in support of the Baltic campaign, but the onslaught was renewed in 1916 and by the end of that year another 1,098 vessels had been sunk. In 1917 the destruction reached a climax with 2,639 ships going down, and in 1918, when the anti-submarine measures of the Allies at last began to turn the tide, the figure was 1,103, making a total of 5,408 vessels lost, with a combined tonnage of 11,189,000 tons.

As the war progressed, however, not only were airships more widely used and in greater numbers, but co-operation between air and sea forces became steadily better. By late 1917 the convoy system had been introduced as the best way of safeguarding shipping, and airships flew out into the Atlantic to meet the convoys, remaining on guard until every vessel was safely in port.

After some initial reluctance, the naval authorities learned to accept the help of the blimps, although they feared at first that the appearance of airships flying above shipping would alert distant submarines to the convoy's approach. This view was soon found to be fallacious and sailors began to appreciate the presence of the blimps, hovering around the ships like sheepdogs with an errant flock. It was not usually possible for an airship to remain with the convoy all the way into port, so they often operated in relays, sometimes with two or three on watch at

"British airships escorting transports", a wash drawing by Algernon Black. Only one vessel was ever torpedoed while being escorted by airships. *Imperial War Museum*

the same time. If only one airship was present she would position herself not ahead of the convoy but to windward, so being able to swoop down rapidly to investigate any threat instead of having to claw her way back against the wind and taking perhaps three times as long to come into action.

The majority of the airships, even towards the end of the war, were still small and restricted in range; even by acting in relays it was possible to escort convoys for only the last 150 miles or so of their long voyage. The airships were further handicapped in many cases by having to fly from bases distant from the scene of operations. To reduce these disadvantages the bold step was taken of mooring out some of these smaller blimps in temporary stations such as old quarries, clearings in woodlands, or other places where there was natural shelter from the wind. This practice began at the end of 1917 and contributed greatly to the success of the 1918 campaign by making the best possible use of the

The R.26, seen here in March, 1918, at her maker's airfield at Barrow-in-Furness, was one of the big rigid airships demanded by so many influential people. Each rigid cost as much as twenty SS Twins.
Royal Aeronautical Society

One of the larger types of non-rigid airship coming into operation in 1917 was the Coastal. Primitive and unlovely though they were, these airships were employed at the right time and in the right places and saw more action than any other type.   *Imperial War Museum*

ubiquitous and invaluable SS Zero ships. At the same time, the larger airships, with their increased range, were coming into service and making a contribution.

In addition to normal duties airships also acted regularly as escorts for the Grand Fleet, although even by the last year of the war their potentialities were still not appreciated correctly by many senior officers. Admiral Beatty, for one, was anxious for the blimps to act as scouts for his fleet, but insisted that they remained in visual contact and did not break radio silence, a prohibition which greatly reduced their usefulness.

Yet it was because of their greater potential for long-range ocean reconnaissance that rigid dirigibles of the Zeppelin type were preferred by many influential administrators and politicians. During all this time the slow progress towards acquiring such airships continued, beset by changes of policy and hesitations as well as by a lack of sheds large enough for their construction and housing. Several Zeppelins were present at the Battle of Jutland in May, 1916, and although it is now known that their presence had little or no influence on events, there was a widespread impression in Britain at the time that it was the scouting abilities of the German airships which had allowed the enemy to evade the British fleet. This belief led to further demands for the rigid airship programme to be accelerated, for at this time no British rigid had yet flown, although No 9 was nearing completion and work had begun on the improved 23 class, consisting of No 23, No 24, No 25, and R.26, the first to use the prefix R.

Government approval had at first been given for six more of the same class to be built, but it was then decided instead that two of these should be the wooden-framed R.31 and R.32, while the other four should be of the new 23X class, consisting of R.27 to R.30. Even this revised plan was further modified, however, for in September, 1916, the naval Zeppelin L-33 was brought down in Essex without loss of life and with very little damage. Close examination soon revealed how inferior were the contemporary British designs. As a result, work on R.28 and R.30 was stopped and instead a new class of sixteen airships, to be based on the L-33 design, was planned, with numbers running—coincidentally-—from R.33 to R.48. In the event, because of the ending of the war, only R.33 and R.34 were built; although they were probably the best airships ever produced in Britain, neither was finished until some months after the Armistice.

In retrospect it is clear that the many changes of policy and direction bedevilled the rigid airship programme and ensured that only eight flew before the war ended. A firm commitment to a modest approach rather than the constant pursuit of an ever-retreating perfection would surely have been more sensible.

It is hard to avoid the conclusion that the Admiralty's desire to develop rigid airships was, at least in part, a matter of national prestige which diverted to the rigid airship programme money and resources that could have been better employed elsewhere. Whatever the theoretical advantages of range, endurance, armament and crew comfort possessed by these large ships, in practice the later SS blimps, particularly those of the Zero and Twin classes, flew longer, further, more often and to greater effect. The total number of hours flown in wartime service by the eight rigids delivered before the Armistice was fewer than 1,525. By comparison, one small blimp alone, SSZ.11, flew 1,610 hours! That this extraordinary contrast was appreciated by those in authority is shown by the fact that there were plans to build over a hundred more of these highly effective little SS airships; the Armistice brought an abrupt end to such ambitious planning.

Nevertheless, the Admiralty also persevered with the rigid airship pro-gramme, despite the fact that each ship of the 23 class cost about £125,000. For this sum it would have been possible to buy some twenty SS Twins or thirty SS Zero blimps: a much better bargain, one would have thought. The suspicion that cost effectiveness was not the only criterion of choice is strengthened by postwar developments; there was a long and determined struggle to keep the prestigious rigid airships in being, but the small and unglamorous non-rigids disappeared with hardly a word of protest. It was fortunate indeed for Britain that the manner in which the wartime airships were deployed was highly efficient, even if the building programme was often misdirected or confused.

CHAPTER SEVEN

The Later SS Airships

D URING the autumn of 1914 another Astra Torres ship was bought by the Admiralty, and she was joined the following year by a third. Six months or so after the war had begun, therefore, Britain still possessed only nine airships, most of which were by then of little real use.

Within less than a year, thanks to the splendid improvisation that had produced the first SS blimps, there were four times as many, and by the end of 1916 the number had risen to around fifty. Although the original SS ships were very successful there was clearly room for improvement in the basic design, and in January, 1917, a slightly different type appeared. This became known as the SSP or "Pusher" class.

All ships of this class were fitted at the rear with 75 hp Rolls Royce or 100 hp Green engines which gave them a top speed of up to 52 mph while shielding the crew from the full force of the slipstream. Of the earlier blimps only those equipped with the Farman-type cars had possessed this advantage. In other respects they were similar to their predecessors, except that a more efficient design enabled them to carry a third crew member, an engineer. One novel feature was the use of rubberized fabric petrol tanks attached to the sides of the envelope, but these were found to be unsatisfactory and were soon replaced by aluminium ones in the same position.

Only six of this class were built, for a few months earlier, in September, 1916, the prototype of an even better small blimp had made her maiden flight at Capel, near Folkestone. She was designed by Flight Lieutenant F. M. Rope and Warrant Officer Righton, encouraged and assisted by their CO, Flight Commander A. D. Cunningham. After Admiral Sir Reginald Bacon, who commanded the Dover Patrol, had given his support the plans were submitted to the Admiralty, who accepted the design gratefully, although only after rebuking the inventors for making unauthorized modifications to naval equipment! The original ship had been known provisionally as SS.0, which led to the new class thus inaugurated being designated as the SS Zero ships. The prototype was deflated in April, 1917, and the car sent to the firm of Frederick Sage and Company of Peterborough to serve as a pattern for the production airships. Four months later, upon its return, the prototype was reinflated and redesignated as SSZ.1, in which form she served until after the end of the war.

The envelope, rigging arrangements and fittings of the new airships were not very different from those of earlier SS airships, but the car was of an original and much improved streamlined type which incorporated seating for a crew of three. It was built up on the triangular girder principle, braced with wire, covered with plywood, further covered with aeroplane fabric and then doped to render it waterproof. Constructed in the shape of a boat, this new car enabled the airships to alight on water and to take off again without difficulty, a facility of which they made good use. (The captain of one Zero class airship made a practice when returning from patrol of coming down alongside any convenient trawler and buying fresh fish for the officers' mess!)

In addition to this improvement, the new ships were found to be more efficient in almost every way than earlier blimps and they became very popular with their crews. They usually carried two 100 lb bombs or one of 250 lb, and were armed with a Lewis gun which was manned by the W/T operator in the front cockpit and could be mounted on either side. The engine was again a Rolls Royce Hawk, a water-cooled engine that was noted for its comparative reliability.

SSZ.23 was commissioned in January, 1918, and flew 336 hours in service at Cranwell and Howden before being sold to the United States in August of that year. *Fleet Air Arm Museum*

The car of SSZ.27 in the hangar at Mullion. A bomb is attached to the starboard side and a net slung below the engine contains a number of other items. *Imperial War Museum*

It was mounted on struts above the rear of the car, to allow better access and to keep it well above water level when the airship came down on the sea. Instead of having to swing the propeller, as on the earliest SS ships, the engineer could now use a starting handle similar to that fitted on motor cars. It turned the engine by means of a chain and sprocket gear, which could also be used to rotate a hand blower and so maintain envelope pressure in the event of engine failure.

The fuel tanks were attached to the sides of the envelope in the same manner as in the previous class. Some of the ships also carried parachutes in cases fixed just forward of the petrol tanks. They had a rather faster rate of climb than their predecessors, reaching a maximum speed of 1,200 feet per minute and ascending at an angle of 43 degrees. They could also dive at 51 degrees, reaching a speed of descent of around 1,400 feet per minute. Their disposable lift was probably rather less than that of the earlier SS ships, but their maximum speed was slightly higher at around 53 mph.

More SS Zero ships were built than of any other class of dirigible in Britain. The first production airships appeared in June, 1917, and no fewer than seventy-seven were commissioned altogether. Despite their late arrival on the wartime scene their record in patrol and convoy work was highly impressive.

The famous "Mullion Twin", SSE.2, was the prototype of a class of airship which would have been built in quantity had the war lasted another year. Commissioned in March, 1918, she flew only 57 hours before being deleted in October, 1919.   *Royal Aeronautical Society*

Several of them flew more than a thousand hours in service, and in 1918 SSZ.11 was in the air for 259 hours during the month of August alone. In the whole of that same year SSZ.20 covered an estimated 28,299 miles in 1,263 hours—all the way round the world at an average 20 knots!

Although they never received the same public acclaim that was so often bestowed upon the undeserving rigid airships, the SS Zero blimps were truly the unsung heroines of the war against the U-boats. Like other SS ships, they showed that enthusiastic amateurs with practical knowledge could find a solution which had eluded the professional designers. Two were sold to France and two to America.

Towards the end of the war two final and interconnected classes of SS airship appeared in an attempt to overcome the ever-present problem of engine unreliability. The agreed solution was to use two engines, either of which would provide sufficient power by itself in an emergency. One attempt, SSE.1 (Experimental), was designed at Cranwell in 1918, but was rejected within two months as unsuitable. About the same time a group of officers at Mullion in Cornwall led by Flight Lieutenant R. S. Montagu produced their own design, which they were given official approval to develop. The result of their work was known as the "Mullion Twin", or SSE.2.

The Mullion Twin was powered by two 90 hp water-cooled Curtiss engines placed on gantries either side of the car. Although she crashed twice, her trials were so encouraging that a new class of SS Twin airships was brought into being based on the same principles. Each of these airships had an enlarged envelope of 100,000 cubic feet capacity, and the twin engines were matched with twin airscoops and four ballonets. They were able to carry a crew of four or five and to cruise at 42 mph for up to 30 hours, with a maximum speed of 58 mph. The longest flight recorded was one of 52 hours by SST.14 between 30th May and 2nd June, 1919.

Had the Armistice not intervened, by the middle of 1919 there would have been an establishment of 115 of these very efficient airships, but the programme was curtailed and only thirteen were eventually produced, the numbers running

Airships often collaborated with surface vessels during their patrols. Here SSZ.37 hovers over the *PC.61*, one of a class of patrol boats built in 1916–17 to resemble small merchant ships. SSZ.37 was based at Pembroke, which was also the home of *PC.61* at the time, and flew 675 hours in service before being deleted in October, 1919. *Imperial War Museum*

from SST.1 to SST.14, with the unsurprising absence of an SST.13. (Oddly enough, there was a SSZ.13—which was wrecked at sea—but all the other classes managed to avoid the number 13 in one way or another.). SST.6 was never officially accepted, since it seems she was delivered with a serious engine fault that caused the ship to catch fire and crash on her maiden flight. Tragically, all five of the crew were killed. Three of the Twins were sold secondhand to America in 1919.

Rather curiously, the last SS ship to be commissioned apart from SST.14 was SSE.3, which was apparently designed and built before the Armistice at Wormwood Scrubs. The Admiralty at first refused to accept her, but for some reason the decision was reversed in early 1919 and she then survived in the RAF until 1921 as a training ship for the American airmen who were to fly in R.38.

Like most of the British wartime airships, the later SS blimps were involved in few spectacular episodes; their very success in deterrence meant that they seldom encountered the enemy. However, there were incidents of both tragedy and triumph.

On 16th March, 1918, due to engine failure, SSP.6 made a forced landing in the sea off Anglesey. The crew were picked up safely, but with the loss of their

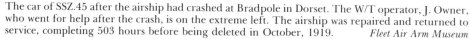

The car of SSZ.45 after the airship had crashed at Bradpole in Dorset. The W/T operator, J. Owner, who went for help after the crash, is on the extreme left. The airship was repaired and returned to service, completing 503 hours before being deleted in October, 1919.   *Fleet Air Arm Museum*

combined weight the airship lifted off again and drifted more than 200 miles before landing in a wood near Chichester, suffering only minor damage.

SSZ.7 had an equally narrow escape from disaster in November, 1917, when sparks from the radio equipment ignited petrol fumes in the car. Despite the proximity of the hydrogen-filled envelope no general conflagration resulted and no serious damage was sustained. It was the more tragically ironic, therefore, that only a month later while returning to Polegate at a low height one foggy night, the same craft, commanded by Sub-Lieutenant R. Swallow, suddenly came upon SSZ.10 which had been moored out as an emergency measure at Jevington, together with SSZ.9, while their crews awaited an improvement in the weather. Sub-Lieutenant Swallow tried vainly to pull SSZ.7 clear, using full throttle and the elevators, but he was too late and the car tore into the envelope of SSZ.10, both airships catching fire as the escaping gas was ignited by the engine exhaust pipe. The W/T operator, Air Mechanic Dodd, and the engineer, Air Mechanic Hughes, flung themselves to the ground, landing badly hurt alongside SSZ.10; the loss of their weight caused SSZ.7 to soar briefly upwards before falling back to earth in flames near to her sister ship. Sub-Lieutenant Swallow perished in the inferno, but rescuers rushed forward to drag clear the two injured airmen and to help those others caught up in the confusion, while two of the ground crew—Air Mechanic Robinson and Air Mechanic Steer—even risked their lives to remove three bombs from the flaming wreckage. They were unable to reach the fourth, which exploded in the heat, seriously injuring Sub-Lieutenant Watson, the captain of SSZ.9, who had returned to help after ensuring that this own ship had been moved away out of danger. These three men all subsequently received awards for bravery.

In August, 1918, SSZ.45 crashed into a hill near Bradpole in Dorset, injuring the pilot, Lieutenant Savage, and the engineer, Air Mechanic Jobson. The W/T operator, J. Owner, was also hurt but he managed to stagger to the nearby post office, where he had the utmost difficulty in persuading the postmistress to allow him to make an emergency telephone call! Happily, help was eventually summoned and before very long both airship and crew were back in action.

On 7th December, 1917, SSZ.16, based at Pembroke and commanded by Sub-Lieutenant F. E. Barrs, was on a routine patrol when she sighted a surfaced submarine about a mile away to windward. The W/T operator, Air Mechanic Tattersall, signalled to base and the airship moved closer to investigate, rising higher as she did so in order to get above the angle of the submarine's gun. As she approached, the submarine altered course towards the airship; Sub-Lieutenant Barrs watched for the British recognition signal, a double spurt of water, as he was not yet certain whether the vessel was an enemy.

Instead came a sudden shot, fired from the gun mounted forward of the conning tower. It missed its target narrowly, and as the blimp swooped in to the

A British submarine signalling its identity to an aircraft by giving a double spout of water, rather like a whale blowing. There was constant concern that an airship might attack a friendly craft. This vessel, *H.9*, was one of a class of ten boats built by Canadian Vickers in 1915; she was in the 8th Submarine Flotilla at Yarmouth until 1918.   *Fleet Air Arm Museum*

attack the W/T operator raked the U-boat's deck with fire from his Lewis gun, sending the German sailors scrambling below.

Within a few minutes the enemy vessel began to submerge, but as the airship came overhead it could still be seen as a light green shape just below the surface of the water. Two 65 lb bombs with delayed fuses were at once dropped close to the submarine's port bow, but only one exploded.

There was no more that could be done, and as the winter's evening was now drawing in and visibility becoming poor two calcium flares were left to mark the spot and SSZ.16 turned for home. On the way—the W/T transmitter having now broken down—she signalled by Aldis lamp to two destroyers racing belatedly to the scene as a result of her earlier message.

Having accomplished the rare feat of actually engaging the enemy, the same airship defied the odds against a repeat performance by finding the oil track of a submarine the very next day. Both bombs were dropped and a nearby trawler which was summoned to the scene added two depth charges to the assault. This time there was greater success, as large amounts of oil came bubbling to the surface, indicating severe damage at least.

Another action on two consecutive days took place in the Irish Sea on 18th and 19th May, 1918. One of three airships patrolling near Bardsey Island saw a narrow stream of oil moving westward. Two bombs were dropped and the other airships quickly joined in the attack, together with a nearby destroyer. After one underwater explosion nothing further was observed and one of the airships, SSZ.35, was able to alight on the sea and take samples of the oil for analysis. The next day the three airships were cruising in the same area in the very early morning when SSZ.51 followed a line of oil bubbles and clearly observed the periscope and hull of a submarine travelling south-west. A 250 lb bomb was at once dropped and an urgent message for assistance sent out. One of the other blimps, SSZ.35, also bombed the spot before three American destroyers and a British destroyer raced to the scene and attacked with depth charges. Oil and debris came flooding to the surface and soon covered a wide area, leaving no doubt that one airship patrol, at least, had gone beyond deterrence to destruction.

It was not the only such occasion, however. Possibly the last action seen by any SS Zero was on 16th September, 1918, when the original SSZ.1, piloted by an American ensign, N. J. Learned, went out on patrol. About seven miles from Capel, a narrow line of oil was seen on the water, stretching out into the distance. For half an hour the airship followed the thin track until it ended in a widening patch, indicating that the U-boat was now stationary. Patrol boats were at once called up to release depth charges over the spot and these were followed by two explosions at once and another a little later. The vessel was later learned to be *UB.103*, one of the last of the 203 German submarines destroyed by British and Allied forces during four years of war.

A general arrangement drawing of an SS Zero airship.

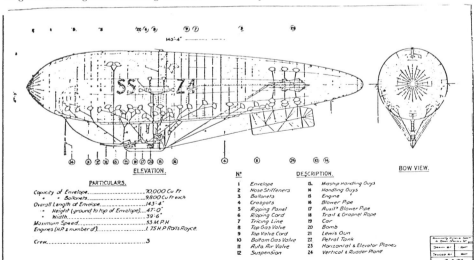

CHAPTER EIGHT

The Coastal Airships

BY THE summer of 1915 the need for airships with greater range, reliability, speed and lift was becoming apparent to the Admiralty, so instructions were sent to Kingsnorth for the preparation of a new type, again making use of existing equipment.

Of the two Astra Torres airships acquired by the Admiralty after the outbreak of war, little is recorded. The first was designated No 8 and was commanded at various times by Commander Hicks and by Commander Usborne. Like her predecessor she was used mainly for patrolling the area of the English Channel and she had an uneventful career before being deleted in May, 1916. The second, commissioned in early 1915, was designated No 10 and had a trilobe envelope with a capacity of some 150,000 cubic feet. She was almost immediately dismantled in order to serve as the basis for the new design, and her component parts were extensively modified in the course of preparation.

An alternative had to be found to the car as this had been specially built before the war for a Belgian millionaire and was made of metal, fully enclosed and with triplex windows. Such a car could not possibly have been reproduced in quantity and at short notice so, mindful once again of the need to use already available material, the development team fell back on an ingenious expedient. Two Avro aeroplane fuselages were obtained and the tail portions, from behind the rear seat, were cut off. The two fuselages were then joined end to end, producing a four- or five-seater car with engine mountings at both ends.

Rather than waste the original Astra Torres car, this was fitted experimentally to the envelope of *Eta*, but the resulting airship, known as *Eta II*, proved unsuccessful and was scrapped after only three flights.

The new type with the improvised car and the Astra Torres envelope was undoubtedly promising, and the prototype was eventually accepted as Coastal class airship No 1 or C.1. She made her final trial flight in January, 1916, and became the first of thirty-five airships (including three rebuilt elsewhere) contracted out to different firms but assembled at Kingsnorth. Four of these were sold to Russia and one to France; the former were known as Ca, Cb, Cc and

The Coastal airship C.27 leaving the shed at Pulham. She had been in service for just a year and had logged 355 hours when on 11th December, 1917, she was shot down by German fighter seaplanes. There were no survivors.

Fleet Air Arm Museum

An early Coastal in the hands of the landing party. The lack of gracefulness is all too evident in this view, but despite basic design faults the Coastals proved extremely useful and saw much action. This example has two-bladed propellers; later ships had four-bladed airscrews.   *Fleet Air Arm Museum*

Cd, while the latter was originally designated C.4, but was renamed Ce upon her transferral and replaced in the RNAS by another C.4.

The design of the production airships was slightly different from that of the prototype, and further minor changes were introduced as experience was acquired. The trilobe envelope was some 196 feet long and had a capacity of 170;000 cubic feet; internally the ridges of each lobe were connected by fabric curtains inserted to help maintain the correct shape but not intended to isolate the three sections. Four ballonets were fitted, two in each of the lower lobes, and a single scoop consisting of a sheet-aluminium tube of oval cross section reached downwards to the forward propeller. Later models used a shorter scoop abaft the after propeller instead, since the original arrangement proved dangerous when landing; not only was the coxswain's vision impeded but the forward engine had to be kept in action to maintain pressure, and this several times resulted in the propeller fouling the mooring ropes and shattering.

In addition to the two engines and the crew accommodation the car also contained oil tanks and a fabric water ballast bag holding up to 85 gallons. This latter was sometimes replaced in later models by bags of sand ballast or was even dispensed with entirely, so making room for an additional crew member. (Petrol was normally consumed faster than gas was lost, so ballast was usually discharged only in an emergency.) The two fuel tanks, each holding 110 gallons, were originally placed also in the car next to each engine, but the later use of the longer Renault engine necessitated the after tank being moved to a position on a superstructure mounted on struts above the engineer's cockpit. Some of the Coastal ships were later fitted experimentally with aluminium tanks slung to the sides of the envelope in a manner similar to that employed in the SSP and Zero blimps. When ballast was not carried petrol could be jettisoned in emergencies.

Single skids replaced the normal undercarriage and also protected the propellers. The rigging was of the normal Astra Torres internal type, and three stabilizing fins were fastened to the rear of the envelope, maintained in position by cables and Eta patches. These carried the rudder and twin elevators, the former controlled by the coxswain in the forward cockpit and the latter by the captain, sitting directly behind him. An observer or second pilot usually sat abaft the captain when the ballast bag was omitted, and the two remaining seats were occupied by the W/T operator and the engineer.

Two 150 hp water-cooled Sunbeam engines were fitted to the proto-type—one tractor, one pusher—but some later models used a 220 hp Renault aft, and in some cases the forward Sunbeam was replaced by another engine, usually a 100 hp Berliet. Compressed air starters were used for the engines, with two air bottles placed on each side of the pilot's cockpit. Spare bottles were carried in the engineer's cockpit. A small 1¾ hp ABC engine was also provided to power the W/T operator's generator. In an emergency it could also be used to operate an auxiliary blower to maintain pressure in the ballonets.

Most airships of the new class were eventually equipped with parachutes. For armament each possessed two Lewis machine-guns, one in the car and one perched precariously on the very top of the envelope. The latter was reached through a vertical fabric tube lined with ash hoops fitted with rungs for climbing. Four bombs of 100 or 112 lb were usually carried, although sometimes depth charges or two 230 lb bombs were substituted.

The Coastal or C class airships were possibly the ugliest dirigibles ever made, with none of the streamlined grace which characterized even the SS ships.

They were also unstable and erratic in flight, sluggish in response to the controls, and a frequent cause of airsickness in their crews. Beyond this lack of beauty or comfort, however, the new design clearly proved to be somewhat disappointing in more vital ways, although there was never any official admission of this.

In common with other British airships, they suffered from frequent engine troubles. Magnetos in particular were most unreliable and engineers became adept at changing them during the course of a patrol, sometimes more than once. Even when working properly the engines produced a speed of only between 45 and 50 mph, no faster than the SS ships, while the one outstanding aspect of the Coastals' performance, a fast rate of climb, was of little value in the work they were called upon to perform.

Their endurance, although theoretically much greater than that of the smaller airships, does not appear to have led in practice to longer or more regular patrols. C.9, it is true, logged more flying hours in service than any other British airship of any class, but although she flew a record 2,500 in an

exceptional career, the largest number of hours flown in one month was 235, compared with SSZ.11's 259. The longest single flight recorded by a Coastal was 24 hours 15 minutes by C.24 on 9th/10th July, 1917. But SSZ.39, piloted by Captain Bryan, remained aloft for 50 hours 55 minutes on 11th/13th August, 1918, and SST.14 flew for 52 hours 15 minutes on 30th May/2nd June, 1919. Again, C.2 averaged 105 miles (3 hours 50 minutes) a day during 1918, but SSZ.51 averaged 115 miles a day (4 hours 15 minutes), albeit over a shorter period.

Of course, the SSZ ships were a later development of their class, but it is perhaps also significant that rather than persevere with the Coastal class and develop it similarly, production ceased in 1916; instead a new type was introduced. Another indication of the Coastal class's failure to achieve all that was hoped for is their high loss rate. Of all types of SS ship retained by Britain during the war—134 in all—only twenty-seven were wrecked, lost at sea or destroyed by fire. Of the remainder, seventy-nine were still in service at the

Opposite page: C.27 being "walked out" of the hangar at Pulham in gusty conditions. The handling party are struggling to hold her steady in the eddies created by the windscreen, which was intended to protect the craft from crosswinds.

Fleet Air Arm Museum

Right: The coxswain at the chart table in C.17, another photograph taken at Pulham.

Fleet Air Arm Museum

A Brandenburg fighter seaplane of the type which shot down C.27 on 11th December, 1917.

Armistice. By contrast, of the thirty Coastals flown by the RNAS, twelve were totally destroyed in some manner and only four survived to the Armistice.

Despite this comparatively poor safety record, which can be attributed in part to encounters with the enemy, the Coastals seem to have seen more action than any other class of British airships, their limitations overcome by the determination and bravery of the men who flew them.

The two most unfortunate of all their class were C.17 and C.27. The former, captained by Sub-Lieutenant E. G. O. Jackson, was patrolling the Dover Straits on 21st April, 1917, when she was attacked by German aeroplanes. Despite fighting back bravely with her machine-guns, the airship stood no chance and was shot down in flames within sight of several trawlers. There were no survivors. The other ship, C.27, commanded by Flight Lieutenant Dixon, was shot down in similar circumstances by two Hansa-Brandenburg seaplanes flying from Zeebrugge on 11th December, 1917. These two Coastals appear to have the sad distinction of being the only British airships destroyed by the enemy during the entire war, although C.25, officially reported as being lost at sea on 31st July, 1918, was also considered by many to have been lost through enemy action. Together with other airships and surface craft, she had been sent out from Longside to search for a U-boat reported as damaged somewhere in the Firth of Forth. Nothing was found, but C.25 alone failed to return and it was conjectured that she had come upon the crippled submarine and been shot down by its deck gun. The Germans never claimed her destruction, but this would be explicable if the submarine had then failed to reach home.

An equally unusual, although happier, fate befell C.26 just a few days after the loss of C.27, for traces of which she was searching. Flying from the same station of Pulham, she lost her way in thick mist over the North Sea and also had problems with the engines. The airship drifted across to Holland, where the captain, Flight Lieutenant Kilburn, brought her down to earth near Dordrecht in the early morning of 13th December. Four of the crew jumped out and tried to anchor the ship, but she blew away, the fifth man falling out as she did so. The airship finally came to rest on top of some houses near Utrecht. The crew were interned.

On 23rd April, 1917, C.11, commanded by Flight Lieutenant Hogg Turnour, was returning to Howden through low clouds when a steep hillside suddenly appeared out of the gloom ahead. The pilot put the elevators hard up and attempted to lift the airship out of danger, but her response was too slow. As the tail dropped, the rear of the car struck the ground and was torn away, and the engine, together with the engineer himself, fell heavily to earth.

Deprived of this considerable weight, the airship shot up into the air some 3,000 feet and the pilot, who was unable to operate the valve, tried to start the ripping panel in order to lose some gas. The internal pressure on the envelope was so great, however, that the panel opened completely, making a long split in the fabric, leaking the gas and sending the ship plunging downwards again. She crashed heavily into the ground, severely damaging the car and badly injuring the three crew members.

Half a mile away on Scarborough racecourse the engineer had escaped with a broken arm. He was able to walk to a post office and send to Howden a message of memorable brevity: "Have landed safely with engine. Request further instructions."

The airship was repaired and back in service within three months, but on 21st July when carrying a crew of six on a routine flight she began to lose height rapidly, for no evident reason. Despite dropping all the ballast and using full engine power, she continued to fall and came down in the Humber; the car sank and the envelope burst into flames as it collapsed on top. Four of the crew were drowned, but the 1st coxswain and the engineer were able to struggle to safety, aided by a man and his fifteen-year-old son who swam out to the wreck. The car, engine and much of the rigging were subsequently retrieved undamaged and C.11 was again repaired, to be finally deleted only in March, 1918.

On 12th February, 1917, C.22, commanded by Sub-Lieutenant C. S. Coltson and on a patrol from Mullion, sighted a Norwegian steamer with boats lowered and the wreckage of another ship a little way off. Two trawlers appeared on the scene and from them, using semaphore, the captain of C.22 learned that the stricken ship had been torpedoed and that a submarine had been sighted briefly. As the rescue proceeded C.22 prowled the sea in search of the enemy.

Some time later C.22 came upon the submarine surfacing about a mile ahead on the port bow. As the airship altered course and swept in to the attack at 1,000 feet the U-boat, with only her conning tower and part of her hull visible, began to submerge again. As the airship flew over, Sub-Lieutenant Coltson dropped a delayed action bomb which struck the deck of the disappearing submarine, just in front of the conning tower, but failed to detonate.

At once the coxswain put the helm hard over and the airship swung round to hover over the swirl left by the receding vessel. Another delayed action bomb followed the first, this time exploding under water and sending large amounts of oil bubbling and frothing to the surface. For another four hours the airship continued to patrol the area, but no further signs of the U-boat appeared and the hunt was eventually abandoned, C.22 returning to base with the hope that the submarine had indeed been destroyed by the second bomb.

On 8th July, 1917, C.14, from Longside Airship Station, was escorting a northbound convoy when she sighted a submarine periscope a mile or so ahead. She at once called up C.10A and C.7 for assistance, but the submarine dived out of sight and was not seen again. As on so many other occasions, the deterrent value of the airships was proved, for the convoy reached port safely without suffering any attack.

Of all the Coastal airships, C.9 had what was certainly the most outstanding

C.20 landing at East Fortune on a day of bright sunshine. Commissioned on 23rd September, 1916, this Coastal airship flew more than 110 hours before being lost at sea on 22nd December, 1917.

career, as well as the one with the most hours flown. Captained at first by Flight Lieutenant J. Struthers, an acknowledged expert in anti-submarine warfare, she became possibly the most famous of all wartime airships, with the greatest number of recorded actions against the enemy. Making her first flight from Mullion, the station best situated for finding and fighting U-boats, on 1st July,

Flight Lieutenant J. G. Struthers with his mascot at Mullion.
Fleet Air Arm Museum

1916, she lasted for two years and seventy-five days before being deleted. In this time she averaged 3 hours 6 minutes in the air every day, flew a total of 2,500 hours 11 minutes and covered an estimated distance of 68,201 miles—a remarkable record when considered against a background of constant mechanical troubles and times when the gas was so contaminated by air that no ballast could be carried out.

On one of her early flights she joined the destroyer HMS *Foyle* for a sweep of the Western Approaches during which she came close to the Channel Islands, where the local troops had been sent a warning to expect the airship. After some nineteen hours in the air the engines broke down completely and Flight Lieutenant Struthers was obliged to come down on the sea near the destroyer, which was able to take the airship in tow. Before reaching Mullion, however, the envelope lost pressure and buckled so badly that the crew had to abandon her. In spite of this she was eventually brought to safety with only slight damage and speedily repaired.

A close examination of the envelope showed several bullet holes. Further inquiry later revealed that the airship had been machine-gunned by the troops in Jersey, who had failed to receive the warning of the airship's impending arrival.

A short time later C.9 was nearing the end of a patrol when she came upon the wreck of a large freighter in a position in which she constituted a considerable danger to other shipping. Flight Lieutenant Struthers called for destroyers to sink the wreck but there was a long wait, during which incorrect D/F bearings were received giving an alleged position somewhere in the middle of Dartmoor. C.9 was twice ordered to return to base, but this the captain refused to do. For nine hours the airship remained in the vicinity until the destroyers, held up by not knowing the correct position, at last arrived to sink the wreckage. The airship's captain escaped any reprimand for disobeying orders; on the contrary, congratulations were sent to the crew by the Admiralty.

On 15th March, 1917, C.9 was on escort duty near Plymouth when further engine trouble occurred. The engineer, Air Mechanic Parkes, found the rear engine actually on fire, with flames reaching up towards the envelope. With considerable courage and presence of mind he smothered the flames by sitting on the engine and at the same time sprayed all around with the fire extinguisher until the blaze was put out. The airship, not for the only time, returned to base on one engine. Subsequent investigation showed that the bolts holding the wooden propeller in place had sheared, and the resulting friction of the shaft had set it alight. Air Mechanic Parkes, it is alleged, had to buy a new pair of trousers out of his wages, as the loss of his old pair was considered to be his own fault!

A month after this incident, on 27th April, C.9 was sent to where a submarine had recently been sighted. Together with trawlers and destroyers she patrolled an area of some hundred square miles for nine hours, constantly on watch. When the captain was just about to call off the search the stern lookout saw a line of foam some four or five miles to the rear. Course was at once altered, Very light signals were fired and W/T calls for help sent out. As the airship drew closer a submarine could be seen diving for safety, disappearing below the surface just before the C.9 could reach her. Bombs were dropped over the spot and a destroyer soon arrived to join in the hunt. Oil was sighted, indicating damage, but destruction was not certain, and worsening weather conditions soon forced C.9 to return home.

Four months after this disappointment perseverance was at last rewarded. One day in September, 1917, C.9 came upon a French steamer which had just been torpedoed and was in serious trouble. Help was immediately summoned and C.9 began to search the vicinity, watching out for any attack on a trawler which was standing by while the steamer waited to be towed to safety. For five hours there was nothing to be seen.

Suddenly a submarine was sighted on the surface about five miles away to leeward. With the wind at her back, C.9 raced to the spot in under five minutes, and although the U-boat had managed to submerge the swirl left by her dive was clearly visible. Two delayed action bombs were dropped just ahead and a violent

C.17 making a forced landing at Pulham. Lack of pressure in the envelope has caused it to buckle; a similar problem caused C.9 to be abandoned by her crew while being towed by a destroyer.

Fleet Air Arm Museum

explosion brought large bubbles of oil and air frothing up to the surface. A destroyer, HMS *Laverock*, and an armed trawler soon arrived to join the search and two more airships, C.2 and C.23A, flew out to help.

Flight Lieutenant Struthers was obliged to go back to Mullion for more fuel and bombs, but C.9 returned within a few hours, by which time the oil patch had spread to cover nearly a square mile of sea. Having been in the air for some twelve hours altogether, C.9 was at last flown back to base, one of the few airships with a realistic claim to have destroyed a U-boat without assistance.

Later the same month C.9 was patrolling her usual beat in very foggy conditions when a ripple was seen on the surface. Closer examination showed a greenish sediment discolouring the water from below, slight traces of oil moving slowly eastward, and indications of disturbance by a propeller. Calcium flares were released to fix the location and armed trawlers nearby were called in to help. C.9 then dropped her bombs, and as the trawlers joined in the attack with depth charges thick oil rose to the surface and all indications of underwater movement stopped. Because of the fog, the position of the suspected U-boat could not be checked by taking bearings, and wireless communication was impeded by nearby cliffs, so a buoy was left to mark the spot. Two other trawlers appeared later to add more depth charges, and a shouted discussion between Flight Lieutenant Struthers and their captains ended in optimistic agreement that the submarine had probably been sunk.

Flight Lieutenant Struthers was eventually awarded the DSC and two bars in recognition of his outstanding achievements. He handed over command of C.9 to Flight Lieutenant T. P. York-Moore on 17th December, 1917, and went to command NS.6 at Longside. C.9 continued her eventful career at Mullion, but was finally deflated on 14th September, 1918, and officially deleted as no longer serviceable on 1st October.

A possibly unique event occurred on 26th December, 1917, when C.23A was escorting a convoy out of Falmouth. Two of the ships were torpedoed, one sinking almost immediately and the other having to be abandoned. A third torpedo missed its target, and by following its track back the airship was able to bomb the U-boat, although without any signs of success. No more attacks followed, however. This was apparently the only known instance of British vessels being sunk while escorted by an airship.

At various times the possibility was explored of increasing the blimps' range of action by refuelling them at sea. Such experiments were carried out with C.1 during the summer of 1916, when she was towed first by the light cruiser HMS *Carysfort* and then by HMS *Canterbury*. After much practice, it became possible for the airship's trail rope to be picked up at some 26 knots before speed was reduced to about 12 knots to allow her to be pulled down to within 100 feet of the cruiser's decks. From there the crew could be changed one at a time by bosun's chair; petrol could be pumped up by compressed air at a rate of 60 gallons in eight minutes. These techniques were not widely used, but on occasion they enabled the Coastal airships to accompany the Grand Fleet as scouts.

General arrangement drawing of a Coastal airship.

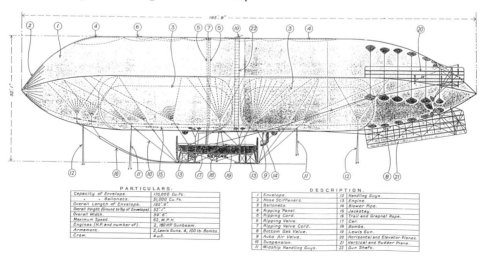

PARTICULARS.	
Capacity of Envelope.	170,000 Cu.Ft.
" " Ballonets.	51,000 Cu.Ft.
Overall Length of Envelope.	185'.9".
Overall Height (Ground to Top of Envelope).	52'.1".
Overall Width.	30'.6".
Maximum Speed.	52, M.P.H.
Engines (H.P. and number of).	2, 150 H.P. Sunbeam.
Armament.	2, Lewis Guns. 4, 100 lb. Bombs.
Crew.	4 or 5.

DESCRIPTION.			
1	Envelope.	12	Handling Guys.
2	Nose Stiffeners.	13	Engine.
3	Ballonets.	14	Blower Pipe.
4	Ripping Panel.	15	Jackstay.
5	Ripping Cord.	16	Trail and Grapnel Rope.
6	Ripping Valve.	17	Car.
7	Ripping Valve Cord.	18	Bombs.
8	Bottom Gas Valve.	19	Lewis Gun.
9	Auto Air Valve.	20	Horizontal and Elevator Planes.
10	Suspension.	21	Vertical and Rudder Plane.
11	Midship Handling Guys.	22	Gun Shaft.

CHAPTER NINE

The C Star Airships

THE LAST and undoubtedly the best of all the British non-rigids were the North Sea airships, but their development was hindered by various mechanical problems. Because the need was great and time short, an interim class of airship which could be produced quickly once again became urgently necessary. This need was admirably fulfilled by the C Star class, hastily produced at Kingsnorth; ostensibly a development of the Coastal class, they were in most important details a new type.

The car, it is true, was basically similar to that of the Coastals—the prototype, indeed, was taken from C.12—and retained open cockpits, but extended engine mounts were put at the rear and the body was covered with plywood instead of fabric. In order to improve observation, four circular portholes of Triplex glass were provided on either side of the car and another window was placed in the floor of the pilot's compartment. Other modifications were carried out to make the accommodation more comfortable for the crew.

Unlike the car, the envelope owed nothing to the Coastal design except a common basis in the Astra Torres trilobe form. The length was increased to 207 feet and the capacity to 210,000 cubic feet. The shape became much more streamlined and graceful than that of the Coastals, although the first three ships still had a rather blunt stern tip; later ships had a slightly more slender tail, increasing the length by another ten feet without adding to the capacity. To improve control and stability, six ballonets were fitted: two large ones amidships, two small ones forward and another two small ones aft. Each pair was connected by a tube, while the three starboard ballonets were further interconnected by the air delivery duct, which led from the airscoop positioned to collect air from the slipstream of the after engine. The duct was fitted externally at first, but was later placed inside the envelope in order to improve the streamlining.

The after engine was a 220 hp water-cooled Renault, while the forward one was a 110 hp water-cooled Berliet. On later models the former was replaced by a water-cooled 240 hp Fiat. As with the Coastal airships, a small auxiliary engine powered the generator, and a fan blower when required.

The petrol storage system was similar to that used later in the North Sea class ships and consisted of four tanks, each of 85 gallons capacity, positioned inside the envelope and slung by bridles from the internal rigging lines. This arrangement gave more space in the car and caused less strain on the suspensions. These main tanks fed two service tanks, each holding 30 gallons, positioned above the car, one to each engine.

There was no gunner's position on top of the envelope, so saving some 250 lb weight and allowing a valve to be placed in that position, but two Lewis guns were carried in the car, which also had fittings for two 230 lb and two 100 lb bombs. Five parachutes were provided, the lines from which could be attached quickly to a harness worn at all times by each crew member.

Although possessing a slower rate of climb than their predecessors, the new ships proved to be superior in every other way and capable of a speed of 56 mph. Nevertheless, they cannot have been regarded as entirely successful, since

The much more elegant shape of the C Star airships is evident from this picture of C*3 over East Fortune; later ships had a more slender tail which further improved the appearance.

although twenty were originally ordered production was discontinued in favour of the SS Twins after ten had been delivered in the six months from February to July, 1918.

In sharp contrast to the Coastal class, the ten C Star airships had generally uneventful careers. They came upon the scene rather late in the war and all of them made long and regular patrols, carrying out their duties efficiently if unspectacularly. The longest continuous flight recorded was one of 34 hours 30 minutes by C*4, commanded by Captain Cleary, on 27th/28th May, 1918.

One novel enterprise in which they might have become involved was a project discussed in August, 1918, to equip all C Star airships with torpedoes for

The car of C*1 was made by modifying and improving that taken from C.12. It was covered with plywood and fitted with portholes of triplex glass. *Fleet Air Arm Museum*

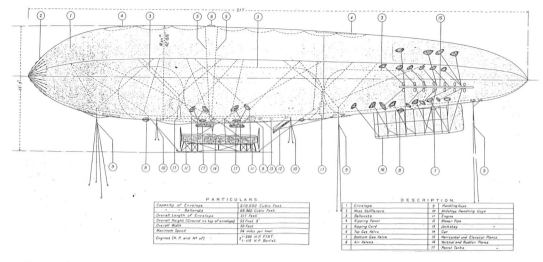

PARTICULARS.	
Capacity of Envelope	210,000 Cubic Feet.
" " Ballonets	68,960 Cubic Feet.
Overall Length of Envelope	217 Feet
Overall Height (Ground to top of envelope)	55 Feet 9"
Overall Width	50 Feet
Maximum Speed	56 miles per hour
Engines (H. P. and Nº of)	1-240 H.P. FIAT. / 1-110 H.P. Berliet.

	DESCRIPTION.		
1	Envelope	9	Handling Guys.
2	Nose Stiffeners.	10	Midships Handling Guys
3	Ballonets	11	Engine
4	Ripping Panel.	12	Blower Pipe
5	Ripping Cord	13	Jackstay
6	Top Gas Valve	14	Car
7	Bottom Gas Valve	15	Horizontal and Elevator Planes.
8	Air Valves.	16	Vertical and Rudder Planes.
		17	Petrol Tanks.

A general arrangement drawing of a Coastal Star airship. The longer, more slender tail of the later ships of this class is shown here.

attacking submarines. As the U-boats frequently submerged no further than periscope depth, it was decided to experiment with circling torpedoes, designed to run in descending spirals. The end of the war prevented the plan from going ahead.

It is also possible that it was a modification of the C Star design which was in the mind of whoever framed the tentative plans to employ airships as flying ambulances. These would have brought urgent medical cases from the Western Front directly to England, escorted by aeroplanes. The proposal, made in January, 1918, was never implemented.

In one respect at least the record of the C Star ships was extraordinary and homogeneous; not one caught fire, was wrecked, lost at sea, or destroyed in any way. None appears to have been involved in any noteworthy incident, all were still active at the time of the Armistice and all were deleted in October of the following year.

CHAPTER TEN

The North Sea Airships

BY 1916 the Government had at last become persuaded that only rigid airships could provide a long-term solution to the problem of finding the ideal anti-submarine aircraft. But although work on a British rigid dirigible had been going on intermittently since 1913, the building of the prototype was proving to be a very protracted affair and the development of improved designs was even further from completion. In these circumstances, the Admiralty decided to order another non-rigid class of airships, which would be simple enough to produce quickly, but large enough to carry two crews in reasonable comfort and sufficient fuel for very long patrols.

The prototype of this new class, to be known as the North Sea or NS airships, was developed at Kingsnorth and was the largest non-rigid designed in Britain up to that time, with a length of 252 feet and a capacity of 360,000 cubic feet, more than double that of the Coastal ships.

There was at first some discussion as to whether the Astra Torres or the Parseval type of envelope would be the better, but the principles behind the design of the latter were not fully understood in this country. Copies could be made—and had been—but any enlargement or modification would require a redesign of the trajectory rigging bands which were a feature of the German airship. This was considered to be a potentially dangerous undertaking, so the Astra Torres pattern which had been adapted without trouble for the Coastal ships was again chosen.

The form used for the new design was not only larger than before but more streamlined, looking quite similar in outline to the SS ships. Six ballonets were fitted, as in the C Star blimps, and four stabilizing fins, of which the lower vertical one carried the only rudder and the two horizontal ones the elevators. A tube incorporating a ladder led from above the control car vertically upwards through the envelope to where a small depression on top provided both a lookout position and a means of egress for the riggers. From there it was possible for them to walk aft all the way to the upper tail fin, inspecting or repairing as necessary. In common with all the other non-rigid airships, a long "ripping panel" was inserted on top of the envelope so that in an emergency the gas could be released instantly.

The enclosed car was made of light steel tubing covered with thin sheets of duralumin and provided with windows and doors. The pilot's cabin was right forward, and behind it were the wireless operator's cabin and sleeping

71

quarters for the crew. Inside the control car were navigation equipment, engine telegraph, speaking tubes and various instruments. There was also a complete electrical system, including two dynamos, batteries, signal lamps and telephones.

From the control car a wooden gangway, supported by cables and sometimes protected by a canvas cover, led aft and slightly upwards to the engineer's car, on either side of which were the two Rolls Royce 250 hp engines under streamlined covers. Floats were attached below the engineer's car as a form of undercarriage.

The armament consisted of two or three Lewis guns in the car and the option of one on top of the envelope, as in the Coastals, but this was rarely fitted. Four or six 230 lb bombs were usually carried, as well as an assortment of smaller ones. There was a total disposable lift of 3.8 tons, almost identical to that of No 9, a contemporary rigid airship which had proved far more expensive and time-consuming to produce. The speed was much higher than that of No 9 at around 56 mph.

NS.1 was completed in January, 1917, but trial flights and modifications

The long propeller shafts which caused so much trouble in the early North Sea ships are plainly seen in this picture of the car of NS.5. The gangway from the control car to the engineer's car is provided with tarpaulin side panels. *Fleet Air Arm Museum*

The first of her class, NS.1 flew 207 hours from her station at Kingsnorth before being wrecked as a result of problems with the faulty engine transmission arrangements.   *Fleet Air Arm Museum*

occupied the next three months and she was not posted to Pulham until April. From there, between 26th and 28th June, she made a flight of 49 hours 22 minutes, at that time a record for British airships of any type. Despite this achievement there were still mechanical problems, and after the first five ships of the new class had been completed there was a pause in production while solutions were found. It was this enforced delay which caused the hasty introduction of the C Star ships.

The chief problem was that in order to enclose and streamline the engines they had been fitted with a complex drive to separate shafts on which the propellers were mounted. Being long, heavy and badly supported, these shafts strained the transmission and usually broke down after about 200 hours. Such trouble was the cause of two of the first five ships, NS.1 and NS.5, being wrecked after forced landings, happily without loss of life. NS.2 had been destroyed earlier, although presumably from a different cause, and these two losses in December, 1917, brought about the immediate grounding of the remaining two North Sea airships.

Two officers at East Fortune, Flight Commander J. S. Wheelwright and

NS.4 after being rebuilt to overcome the mechanical problems which had caused the loss of NS.1 and NS.5. Stationed first at East Fortune and then, after the rebuild, at Longside, NS.4 flew 265 hours during an uneventful career that ended when she was deleted in October, 1919.

Fleet Air Arm Museum

Lieutenant-Commander A. S. Abell, the Engineer Officer, then produced their own plans for reconstructing the ships. By the end of January, 1918, permission had been received and the modifications began at once. NS.3 was chosen and the two Rolls Royce engines were replaced by two 240 hp Fiat engines driving the airscrews direct.

Other changes were also made, including an alteration in the siting of the aluminium petrol tanks, which at first had been placed above the side lobes of the envelope. These were now hung inside the envelope to improve both the streamlining and the weight distribution. In addition, a further modification now allowed the engineer to switch from one tank to another directly from his seat instead of having to climb on to the top of the envelope. As a result of all these changes it became possible to raise the control car level with the engineer's car. The two cars were then faired together by a canvas-covered framework, producing what was in effect a single streamlined unit.

After two very successful trial flights on 11th and 12th March, during the second of which NS.3 remained in the air for eight hours and reached a speed of

60 mph, the Admiralty was fully satisfied. The same modifications were carried out to NS.4, and production of more ships to the revised design went ahead, although apparently not with all the minor improvements to the cars carried out on NS.3 and NS.4.

The long delay had had its effect, however, for not until the last day of May was the next North Sea ship, NS.6, delivered to Longside. Another seven followed before the Armistice and one more just afterwards, making fourteen in all. The series ended with NS.16; it seems that an NS.15, NS.17 and NS.18 were also constructed, but with the end of the war they were neither delivered nor accepted. In deference to the usual prejudice, there appears to have been no NS.13, unless she was also built but not commissioned.

The North Sea airships came into the war in their modified form too late to have any decisive effect on the conflict. Nonetheless, they proved to be very efficient. The crew of ten included pilot, co-pilot, two coxswains, two W/T operators, two engineers and two gunners. The coxswain on duty controlled the steering of the ship by means of a wheel while the pilot, apart from being the officer in overall charge, manipulated the elevator wheel and watched the gauges carefully to check on gas pressure in the envelope. The gunner on duty also acted as cook and helped in other ways as ordered.

Not only did the airmen now have the comfort of enclosure, but there was rest, sleep and even cooked meals, provided by placing a saucepan on the flanged steel plate welded to one of the exhaust pipes. The dirigible could remain at sea for days if necessary, with the men alternating spells of duty. If an engine broke down, it was possible to maintain a reasonable speed with the remaining one while repairs were undertaken. To enable such work to be carried out the sides of the engineer's cabin hinged downwards to form counters that were used as workbenches. The commonest source of trouble appears still to have been the magnetos.

Several of the flights made by the North Sea ships were quite extraordinary by previous standards and included at least nineteen of more than 24 hours' duration. The longest was the world record of 100 hours 50 minutes put up by NS.11, piloted by Captain Warneford, in February, 1919. Together with NS.12, she also made the first airship flight from Scotland to Norway just after the Armistice. Such protracted and reliable flights, carried out in safety and in reasonable comfort, show what the North Sea airships might have achieved had they come upon the scene much earlier and in greater numbers. As it was, they were involved in much drama.

NS.3 was the first of her class to re-enter operational service following her rebuilding, and on 20th April, commanded by Flight Commander Wheelwright, she completed a 55 hour flight escorting convoys. She began by carrying 800 gallons of fuel, 60 of oil and 50 of ballast, in addition to three 230 lb bombs, three Lewis guns, a crew of ten and an American observer, Ensign Behr. The crew worked in alternate watches and complained only of an insufficient supply of fresh water and of sleeping bags which were unlined.

On 9th May the airship alighted on the sea in order to hail a trawler. Not realizing that the airship was being blown backwards, the trawler came up astern, nearly causing a collision. Only by dropping ballast and rising sharply into the air was NS.3 able to escape disaster, the damage being limited to the tail fin, which had been snagged by the trawler's mast. On a subsequent occasion she again alighted on the water during towing trials with the destroyer HMS *Vectis*. These showed that the airship could be towed safely at some 20 knots and that it was possible to transfer personnel or other items.

On the evening of 21st June, 1918, NS.3 left East Fortune on convoy duty, but she encountered very strong winds and was compelled to turn back to seek safety at her base. All through the night she forced her way south, but by daybreak the wind had increased to about 40 knots and NS.3 was still some way from home and crawling along over the Firth of Forth. The ship was being heavily buffeted, making it increasingly difficult to maintain the envelope in its correct shape, and the co-pilot, Flight Lieutenant P. E. Maitland, had alternately

NS.7 being walked into her shed. Commissioned in June, 1918, and based at East Fortune, this airship watched over the surrender of the German fleet in November that year. She and SSE.3 were the last British non-rigid airships in service, both being deleted early in 1921.

to lower the airscoops and to pull on the valves as the pressure varied wildly from one minute to the next. At the same time the pilot was struggling with the elevator wheel, trying to keep the ship level and at a safe height above the waves.

Suddenly, not far from Dunbar and about three miles from shore, the ship began to fall, driven down by the force of the gale in spite of full engine power. Her bows pointing steeply upward, she struck the sea with an impact that tore off the engine car, which sank immediately. The loss of this considerable weight aft caused the ship to soar again into the air, with her nose now tilted sharply downwards. All those members of the crew left in the control car clung on desperately, knowing that there was no hope left for the airship and little for themselves. Commander Wheelwright shook hands with the coxswain, and as the W/T operator attempted to signal for help with the Aldis lamp, the ship dipped to the vertical, gas poured out through rents in her envelope and she hovered momentarily before plunging into the water. The two engineers had already gone down with the engines; now the coxswain, a gunner and one of the W/T operators also drowned, caught up in the tangle of wreckage. The other five men struggled clear and were able to scramble on to a flat part of the envelope, where they held on grimly as it slowly sank beneath them. Mercifully, a destroyer arrived in time to pick up the survivors. What was left of the airship was sunk by gunfire.

NS.9 was posted to Longside after completing her acceptance trials at the end of July, 1918. Not long afterwards, while patrolling near Aberdeen, she was shot at by a submarine hidden from view in the haze. Only minor damage was sustained, but the danger had been no less real for being unusual; without warships in support nearby, an unwary airship presented an easy and vulnerable target to any submarine cruising on the surface with its guns manned.

On 21st September NS.9 returned from patrol, following NS.10 towards the airfield in the teeth of a strong and blustery wind. Both airships proved too much for the landing party to handle in the gusty conditions, and after they had failed to reach safety in the hangar, both had to be ripped. Normally this procedure would have involved only a routine repair of the envelopes and then reflation before a return to active duty. Presumably on this occasion there was further damage of some sort, for although the two airships were sent off to Kingsnorth for repair they did not return and were officially deleted on 3rd October.

Of the other North Sea ships, NS.14 was sold to America, NS.16 was not delivered until January, 1919, and NS.11 met possibly the saddest fate of any British airship. Having survived the war, broken the world's endurance record and made many other exceptional flights, she was travelling along the Norfolk coast near Cley on 15th July, 1919, when as she passed beneath a long black cloud some way offshore she was seemingly struck by lightning. The airship exploded with a vivid flash, killing Captain Warneford and all on board.

CHAPTER ELEVEN

The Parseval Airships

O F THE seven airships with which Britain went to war in 1914, five were flown infrequently if at all after the first few months. The Willows training ship, No 2, appears to have been discarded early on, while *Beta*, *Gamma*, *Delta* and *Eta* were soon used only for training duties. Later they were deflated and remained in store for many months until collectively deleted as unserviceable, together with No 3 and No 8, the Astra Torres ships, in May, 1916.

Only No 4, the Parseval, remained in flying condition, giving faithful service to her adopted country for much longer and flying successively from Kingsnorth, Howden and Pulham. She was well known to soldiers crossing to France, for under the command of Flight Lieutenant G. H. Scott she frequently accompanied the transports and ensured their safety. Apart from the North Sea class airships, she was much larger than any of the native British non-rigids, yet with a very well designed envelope.

Two more of her type were to have been built by Vickers and a third was ordered from the same firm by the Admiralty as a replacement for the one which was not delivered from Germany because of the onset of war. Despite the designation of the latter as No 5 and the other two as No 6 and No 7, the construction of all three was long delayed due to other and more essential war work. They were all slightly larger than No 4, being 301 feet long and with a capacity of 364,000 cubic feet. In each case the nose was stiffened with thin steel tubes and the weight of the car was distributed over the whole of the envelope by trajectory bands, which also served to strengthen the fabric and to maintain the gasbag in shape without the need for excessive inflation pressure. The two ballonets had a total capacity of about 110,000 cubic feet and this allowed the airships to reach heights of up to 10,000 feet. As with the Coastal airships, a gun platform was fitted on top of the envelope and reached by an access tube.

No 5 was belatedly completed, albeit with a Coastal type car, in 1917, and made her first flight in November. The other two had enclosed cars made of duralumin, each containing two 180 hp Maybach engines driving swivelling propellers, a device still being used by the new British rigids then coming into service, but generally regarded by that time as an obsolete and unnecessary complication. Ballast and fuel were carried in the car and an air blower to inflate the ballonets was provided, to be driven either from the main engines or from a small auxiliary engine that also powered the dynamo.

No 6 first flew in December, 1915, but was then dismantled before being

Although slightly larger than No 4, the Parseval No 6 was built by Vickers to the same plan. The trajectory rigging bands formed a distinctive feature of the design and permitted a certain amount of movement to the car, so damping out some of the pitching caused by any sudden change of trim. The car of No 6, below, was comparatively short and had to be slung well below the envelope. It was made of duralumin, with triplex windows, and contained the ballast, fuel and oil as well as the engines. *Imperial War Museum*

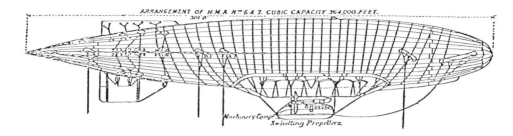

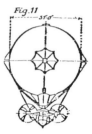

General arrangement drawing of HMA No 6 and No 7, the Parseval airships built by Vickers.

sent to Howden for reassembly. The other two were also assembled at Howden, the components being sent by rail from Barrow, and all three ships were specially strengthened in order that inexperienced ground crews should not be able to inflict damage.

The original ship, No 4, was the first to go, being deleted on 17th July, 1917, as no longer serviceable. No 7 was deleted and broken up for spares in March, 1918, while No 5 was scrapped for similar reasons in the following July. This left only No 6, which flew 428 hours altogether in service. Her last few flights were in the spring of 1919, when she patrolled the North Sea in search of mines. She was deflated in May but not officially deleted until October, the same date which saw the end of so many other airships.

CHAPTER TWELVE

SR.1

THE ITALIAN-BUILT SR.1 was unique; she was the only semi-rigid airship ever owned by the Admiralty.

In 1914 there had been a proposal to buy three Forlanini airships from Italy, but the outbreak of war prevented such an acquisition. Several British airships were sold to Italy during the war and it was possibly to redress the balance that in 1918 the British Government rather surprisingly decided to buy a semi-rigid of the Italian M class, to be designated SR.1. A British crew, led by Captain George Meager, was sent out to Rome, where they carried out trials and accustomed themselves to the new airship in August, September and October.

She was larger than any British non-rigid, being 270 feet in length, 55 feet in diameter and 441,000 cubic feet in capacity. The envelope was supported at its base by a horizontal framework of triangular-section girders of tubular steel. At regular intervals on the two longitudinal girders were fastened parabola wires which looped from end to end and secured the lower edges of the envelope. From the same points lift wires led up inside the envelope and were connected to parabola wires in the two internal fabric curtains that were themselves fastened to the top of the envelope by suspension wires. A ballonet ran along the entire lower length of the envelope and was inflated through a valve at the nose, which operated in a manner similar to that of a Venetian blind.

The single car, of squat and angular form, contained three engines: a single SPA and two Italas, which were actually German Maybachs built on licence; these gave the ship a top speed of 46 mph. A crew of nine was normally carried.

SR.1 left Rome in the early hours of 28th October, arriving in the afternoon at Aubagne in the south of France, having flown across the Ligurian Sea between Corsica and Elba. The airship was moored in the open, as the hangar was found to be too small to take her, and she left very early the following day after refuelling. For this leg, the ship carried an extra crew member: a French airman who assisted with the navigation. As the SPA engine gave constant trouble, and headwinds further slowed the ship during the morning, she was landed at Bron, near Lyons, instead of pressing on to Paris. It was not a regular airship station but simply an emergency landing ground, so the airship was perforce tethered to a heavy lorry while refuelling and maintenance were carried out. The flight was resumed next day and good progress made in spite of further troubles with the engines, including the loss of a complete exhaust pipe. St Cyr near Paris was reached in about ten hours, but again the hangar was too small, so once more the ship had to be moored in the open. Fortunately the weather remained good and for the third night running conditions were calm. The final leg across the English Channel to Kingsnorth was completed in eight hours on 31st October, making a total time for the journey of 40 hours 35 minutes. It was the first flight by any form of aircraft between Italy and Britain, either way.

Six days later SR.1 was flown to her allotted station at Pulham, where the unreliable SPA engine was removed. The war had only five days left to run and SR.1 was never used operationally except when she watched over the surrender of the German U-boats at Harwich.

She flew over London on 2nd July, 1919, as publicity for the War Loan. A similar flight over South Wales followed on 6th and 7th July and a month later a final demonstration flight was put on for the benefit of visiting regiments from India.

A month later she was deleted: an airship clearly inferior to contemporary British dirigibles and of interest only because of her one noteworthy exploit and her unusual design.

The SR.1 was the only semi-rigid airship ever owned by the Admiralty and the first aircraft to fly from Italy to England.
Royal Aeronautical Society

CHAPTER THIRTEEN

HMA No 9

THE GERMAN Zeppelins inspired a respect and fear in Britain out of all proportion to the actual damage they were capable of causing. By the standards of later wars, their bomb loads were small and their navigation extremely bad, yet many people in both Germany and Britain believed that they could win the war almost unaided.

The Germans therefore persevered with their bombing raids even as their casualties mounted horrifyingly, and when a dispassionate assessment would surely have shown them that they were only squandering a vital asset. Similarly, even in England, there were those who believed that Britain should also build large rigid airships. Although few wished to use them in bombing raids in the way the Germans had, it seemed obvious that with their greater range and weight-carrying ability they would be able to scout, patrol and escort more effectively than the small blimps.

One rigid was already in course of preparation even before the outbreak of war, but the work had proved remarkably protracted. The original order had been given to Vickers in June, 1913, and the contract was confirmed the following March. It was stipulated that the airship should attain a top speed of 45 mph, carry a minimum load of five tons (later reduced to 3.1 tons) and be able to reach an altitude of 2,000 feet, remaining at that height for at least half an hour. She should also be capable of carrying two Maxim guns on top of the hull and a one-pounder in each of the two cars. Even by pre-war standards these were modest requirements, except possibly the very last, but this did not make for fast completion. Work had barely begun when war was declared, and there was a hiatus after Winston Churchill cancelled the project at the beginning of 1915 until Arthur Balfour ordered work to begin again in July of the same year. Even then matters proceeded very slowly, for many of the technicians at Vickers had been dispersed and the designers, H. B. Pratt and Barnes Wallis, had actually been recruited into the Army. All of these had to be located and brought together again before the work could recommence.

The two designers had based their airship partly on the experience gained with HMA No 1, the *Mayfly*, but also on what had been learned of later German practice. Much of the available information was supplied by the French after the German Army Zeppelin Z-4 had suffered engine trouble and had mistakenly landed at Luneville in April, 1913. The development of No 9 was marked by none of the speedy improvisation that characterized the building of the non-rigids, and matters were further impeded by a labour demarcation dispute and the Irish rebellion, which prevented early delivery of flax required for the netting to protect the gasbags. Not until the autumn of 1916, more than three years after the order had been first placed, was No 9 at last completed.

Her longitudinal profile was a modified form of the parallel-sided "Zahm" shape used on No 1, with the radius of the bow being twice the diameter of the parallel portion, but the stern being only six times the diameter instead of nine. She was 526 feet long overall, with an extreme width of 53 feet and a height of 76½ feet.

Her frame was constructed almost entirely of triangular-section girders formed of narrow duralumin channel, the running members braced together by diagonals. The longitudinal girders were 8.0 inches in depth and 5.2 inches wide at the base, while the girders of the transverse frames were very slightly smaller. The whole shape was kept taut by steel wiring and had the cross section of a seventeen-sided polygon with the two lowest longitudinal girders in the same horizontal plane. Within this framework, separated by the transverse frames and their radial wiring, were seventeen compartments, each of which contained its own appropriately shaped gasbag made of rubber-proofed cotton fabric lined with three layers of goldbeater's skin obtained specially from America; some 350,000 skins, from as many animals, were required for each wartime British rigid airship. Each gasbag was fitted with two automatic valves, one of which could also be operated by hand. The total gas capacity was some 846,000 cubic feet, giving a gross lift of about 25 tons. This lift was distributed evenly throughout the framework by nets connected to the longitudinal girders; these prevented the material of the gasbags from chafing against the metal.

From the two lowest girders was suspended a keel of tubular construction and triangular section, forming a strong corridor which gave added strength to the airship's structure and also acted as a depository for ballast, fuel tanks and other items, as well as being a means of communication between the cars. Half way along, the keel was widened to form a trapezium-shaped space in which was accommodated the crew's quarters and a wireless telegraphy cabin.

A climbing tube near the bows led up from the keel corridor to a gun platform on top of the airship, from where it was possible to clamber down the top walking-way to the tail. As with later rigid airships, it was even possible to move along the walking-way while the ship was in flight. Most men crawled carefully, keeping a firm hold on the rope positioned alongside, but the riggers themselves usually took pride in walking upright and unsupported, despite the force of the airstream. The trick consisted of leaning forwards when walking towards the bows, and backwards when going aft.

At the stern of the ship were fitted vertical and horizontal stabilizing fins. Below the latter were attached on each side triplane rudders and biplane elevators, while further forward on each side were auxiliary biplane rudders.

His Majesty's Airship No 9 in her modified form with a single engine in the rear car in place of the two originally fitted. Her "Zahm" shape gave her an air resistance equivalent to sixteen per cent of a hypothetical flat disk of the same diameter, so producing twice the drag of contemporary Zeppelins.
Fleet Air Arm Museum

The whole framework was covered with linen fabric, doped for tightness and over most of its area impregnated with aluminium dust, except where special fireproof fabric was used above the engines and near the gun platform.

Beneath the keel were suspended the two cars or gondolas, each about 30 feet long and both containing a control room forward and two 180 hp Wolseley Maybach engines aft. Each engine drove its own propeller mounted on an outrigger and swivelling as required to provide vertical control. Handling rails, buoyancy bags and two landing wheels were fitted to both cars, which had additionally been made watertight so that the airship might alight on water if necessary.

When at long last No 9 was ready for her lift and trim tests these proved very disappointing. At the insistence of the Admiralty, who were afraid their new airship might be damaged by inexperienced ground crews, she had been built with much greater strength than was either necessary or desirable. The result of this unwise condition was that she was found to be at least a ton heavier than had been expected and did not have even the modest 3.1 tons of disposable lift stipulated in the revised contract. Only about two tons were available for ballast, fuel, crew, armament and other items. (By comparison, the Zeppelins of the L-30 class, already in service, could each lift around 28 tons—Z-4 had been old-fashioned even in 1913!)

There was no disagreement between the officials and the designers that drastic modifications and lightening were urgently needed. However, it was agreed that a trial flight before changes were attempted would detect any other faults and allow them to be rectified at the same time. Accordingly, a few days later on 27th November No 9 was walked out from the hangar, breaking off both the wheels beneath the forward gondola as she hit a railing. Despite this setback, a crew of sixteen, captained by Wing Commander A. E. D. Masterman and including H. B. Pratt, the designer, went aboard, and not long after 10 am the airship lifted off cleanly and headed for the open sea. Within minutes, however, things went wrong with the auxiliary rudders as their control wires stretched and became displaced, allowing them to flap from side to side. With some difficulty these were eventually secured and No 9 cautiously made her way over Walney Island and Morecambe Bay, keeping to a height of about 900 feet and a speed of 35 mph. Her handling was quite acceptable, except that the steering was now rather ineffective without the use of the auxiliary rudders, so after half an hour the ship was turned slowly round, to arrive back at Barrow just after 11 am. The first attempt to land failed when excessive lightness caused her to rise abruptly as she slowed down, but a leisurely circle brought her back again over the field. As the trail rope was dropped, gas was valved and the propellers swivelled to force her downwards into the hands of the landing party.

The Admiralty officials were clearly unhappy about No 9's lack of performance, but they realized that only minor improvements were possible,

Schematic drawings of HMA No 9, showing the rear car as modified but also including the auxiliary rudders which were removed during early trials at Barrow.

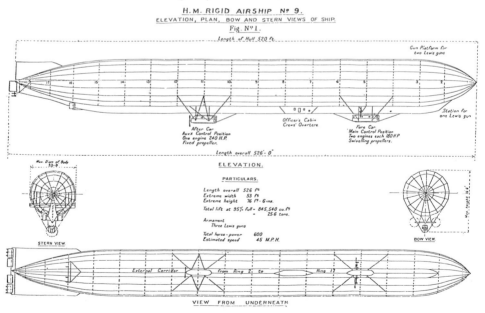

and after considerable discussion it was agreed that the ship would be accepted officially on 12th December, but only on the understanding that she could then reach the specified speed and that modifications leading to an increase in the disposable lift would be carried out without delay. The day following this provisional acceptance, speed trials were held, although this time Barnes Wallis was a passenger instead of H. B. Pratt. The airship made her way northwards and was circling slowly in order to fly south over Walney Island when the auxiliary rudders again broke free, as on the previous occasion. Once more they were secured, but the trial was abandoned and No 9 returned to Barrow and to a heated discussion. Barnes Wallis appears to have won the argument; he spent his lunch break personally supervising the entire removal of the auxiliary rudders and their ancillary equipment. In the afternoon another flight took place, when the steering showed a modest if not spectacular improvement and a top speed of 42.5 mph was reached, still somewhat slower than had been specified.

At the beginning of the new year No 9 was laid up and modified as extensively as possible in order to reduce her weight. The most radical alteration was the removal of the two engines in the rear car with their propellers and their replacement by a single 250 hp Maybach engine which had been salvaged from the wrecked German L-33. This drove one slightly larger propeller; to accommodate it the car had to be suspended lower than before. Other items were removed or drastically lightened, the most effective measure being probably the remaking of the gasbags with only two instead of three layers of goldbeater's skin; this modification alone saved nearly seven hundredweights.

All this work took more than two months to complete, but on 17th March, 1917, No 9 was at last ready. The lift and trim trials showed that the changes had proved their worth; the disposable lift was 3.8 tons, nearly double what it had been before and 0.7 tons more than the contract specification, although still no better than that of the North Sea non-rigids which were soon to enter service. The ship was slightly nose heavy, but extra ballast provided a temporary cure.

Commander W. Hicks took her up for her final trial on 23rd March, carrying twenty-one passengers and crew. No 9 handled reasonably well and in spite of the reduced engine power managed a top speed of 43 mph, with which the Admiralty officials had to be content. Only minor matters, including the fitting of a fuel tank aft to balance the trim, required attention and on 4th April No 9 finally entered service, nearly four years after the original order had been placed. Captained again by Commander Hicks, she left Barrow at 11.20 am and made her way across Carnforth into Yorkshire, where she ran into a heavy snow squall and strong winds that forced her towards the ground, her bows pointing steeply downwards. The engines were stopped briefly to allow her to regain the correct trim, and after releasing nearly half a ton of water ballast she climbed to 2,000 feet to escape the storm and make the remainder of her way safely to Howden, where she arrived at 2.45 pm.

A large ground handling party stands by on the field as No 9 flies over Howden. By this time the landing wheels under the forward car had been removed. *Fleet Air Arm Museum*

There, captained usually by Commander Masterman, she was employed mostly in training and experimental work. Her wheels, which had given constant trouble, were soon replaced by bumping bags. The armament was fitted at Howden; this consisted of two Lewis guns and only three bombs, each of 100 lb—a load little heavier than that carried by an SS blimp. In spite of being so weak in both defence and attack, at least one operational flight took place, on 21st and 22nd July, when Flight Lieutenant G. H. Scott was in command. An uneventful patrol over the North Sea saw no incidents and No 9 returned for a safe night landing after being in the air for 26 hours 45 minutes.

Later in the year the airship was put through turning trials which showed that she was both erratic and clumsy. On one occasion she actually swung momentarily in the opposite direction to that steered, but even when turning correctly she proved to be unpredictable. At a steady speed of 17 knots she completed a full circle with a radius of a mile when turning to starboard, but did so with a radius of only just over half a mile when turning to port. An increase in speed brought about some tightening of the circle, but even at 34 knots she took more than five minutes to complete a circle of about three miles circumference. A hostile submarine, had one ever been encountered, would have had little difficulty in evading an attack.

During her later service career No 9 was stationed also at East Fortune, Cranwell and Pulham. Although mainly a training ship, she was also used to test various anchoring methods including a new "three wire system", being moored to a drogue in the Wash and being towed by an Army tank fitted with a short mast. On one occasion a blustery wind is said to have caused her to lift the tank bodily into the air. Finally, after lying idle in her hangar at Pulham for three months, she was deleted and scrapped on 28th June, 1918, when the commanding officer at Pulham, Captain F. L. M. Boothby, retained 20 feet of her nose framework for use as a rose trellis and bandstand.

No 9's total flying record in service was 4,508 miles in 198 hours 45 minutes. She had the distinction of being the first British rigid airship to fly, but whether her contribution to the war effort was worth all the time and money spent on her is extremely doubtful; she was built too heavy, too slow, too unwieldy and, above all, too late.

The forward car of No 9, with E. A. D. Masterman leaning from the window. The ground crew hold on to the handling rails to keep the airship steady.　　　　　　　　*Imperial War Museum*

CHAPTER FOURTEEN

The 23 Class

A T THE same time that work on No 9 was resumed in June, 1915, an order was given to Vickers to produce a more advanced type of airship, incorporating improvements suggested by experience and by later acquired knowledge of German development. A top speed of 55 mph and a disposable lift of 8 tons were specified.

The design work proceeded quickly, for in essence the new ships were merely modified versions of No 9, with an extra bay inserted in the middle and the ends widened in order to contain eighteen gasbags with a total capacity of 942,000 cubic feet, giving a gross lift of some 28½ tons. They were each 535 feet in length, 53 feet wide and with a maximum overall height of 75 feet. The tail surfaces were much simpler in arrangement than those of No 9 and consisted of two vertical and two horizontal fins, to which were attached two rudders and two elevators respectively.

A gun platform was incorporated on the top of the hull and this was intended to take a two-pounder gun and two Lewis machine guns. The platform was surrounded by 18 inch high stanchions carrying a protective life line. At the front, the stanchions could be extended to twice the height and provided with a canvas windscreen. Three other Lewis guns were also to be fitted—at the extreme tail, in the control car and further aft on the top walking-way. The bomb load, although to be greater than that of No 9, was not specified in detail.

The ships each possessed an external keel, of the same pattern as that fitted to No 9, in which a keel cabin of trapezium cross-section was similarly incorporated. This cabin, about 45 feet long, was intended to contain a bomb room, officers' quarters, men's quarters, wireless room and a lavatory aft. From the keel were suspended three cars or gondolas, accessible by open ladders. The forward car was 30 feet long overall and was partitioned into two compartments, a control room forward and an engine room aft. Standing in the control room, like his nautical counterpart on the bridge, the officer in command seldom took the controls himself. Instead, he gave his orders to the steering coxswain, who operated a centrally placed wheel controlling the rudders, and to the elevator coxswain, who controlled the ship's attitude by means of another wheel, set to one side. Toggles to release the water ballast were close to hand, as were lines to the gasbag valves and a telegraph communicating with the various engine rooms. That in the forward car contained a 250 hp water-cooled Rolls Royce Eagle engine, Series 3, fitted with a starting handle and driving a pair of swivelling four-bladed propellers, 10 feet in diameter, through gears.

The after car was the same size as the forward car and was similarly equipped, except that the control room was intended for emergency use only. The midship car was smaller and consisted only of an engine room that contained two engines of the same type as the others, each of which drove its own fixed 11-foot-diameter four-bladed propeller mounted alongside on brackets.

There were twenty fuel tanks in the keel, each with a capacity of 60 gallons, and these fed to service tanks in each of the three cars. There were also twelve water ballast bags in the keel, each of 28 gallons capacity, and two similar-sized

No 23 is carefully walked across the field at Pulham by a large ground party. The tank was converted to act as a movable mooring tower. *Imperial War Museum*

bags in each gondola. The usual mooring and handling ropes were fitted and airtight buoyancy bags were placed beneath the floors of the gondolas for use if the airship should have to alight on water.

A crew of sixteen was normally carried, with provision for two supernumeraries if required. In common with other large British airships, ships of the 23 class carried in the keel during active service a wickerwork cage containing a pair of carrier pigeons. Should the W/T transmitter fail they would provide a last chance of communication with the airship's base.

No 23 alone was provided with two parachutes for experimental purposes. They were of the "Spencer" type; each was folded up and packed in a special case, one positioned on the keel cover next to the central cabin and one below the handling rail of the forward gondola. A long attachment cord led from each parachute into the gondola and ended in a clip that could be fastened quickly to a harness worn by the user. The open edges of each case were held together with thin thread which would break and release the parachute when sufficient weight was applied to the attachment cord. A trial with a dummy proved successful, but the apparatus was apparently never used otherwise.

The designs for the new class were approved by the Admiralty in October, 1915, and Vickers began work at once on the first of these, No 23, which gave her name to the class. Plans were also sent to Beardmore's of Glasgow and

Schematic drawings of No 23, erroneously described on the drawings as "R.23"; it was only on 18th December, 1917, that the Admiralty decided that all future rigid airships should have the prefix R, and the first to bear this designation was R.26.

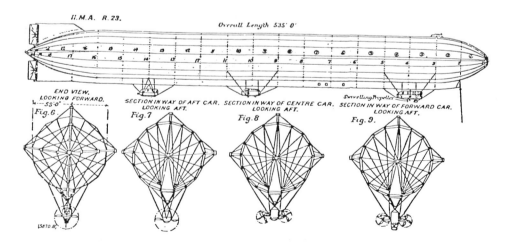

Captain Little releasing a carrier pigeon from No 23. These birds were carried for emergency use in all large airships. The bulkhead behind him bears an interesting submarine identification chart.

Fleet Air Arm Museum

Armstrong Whitworth for them to build No 24 and No 25 respectively. A fourth ship, R.26, was ordered a few months later, to be built by Vickers when space became available. In April, 1916, Governmental approval was given for a total fleet of ten 23 class ships to be produced eventually, but this plan was later modified in the light of subsequent events, the other six becoming four of the 23X class and two of the R.31 class.

No 23 was the first of the new class to be completed—about a year later than promised—and at her lift and trim trials on 26th August, 1917, she was found to have a disposable lift of only 5.7 tons, due to the machinery weight being more than two tons heavier than originally estimated. Five weeks later No 25 was also completed and her tests gave an almost identical result. Although not entirely unexpected, these figures were disappointing, and a fortnight later on 18th October a conference at the Admiralty decided, following the precedent of No 9, that the design must be altered. On the very day this decision was made No 24 was also tested and found mysteriously to be nearly two-thirds of a ton heavier than her sister ships, with a disposable lift of only 5.1 tons.

The Admiralty ordered that modifications be carried out at once to R.26, which was still in the early stages of construction, while the other three ships were to be modified similarly but, of necessity, over a longer period and slightly less drastically. The measures to be undertaken were aimed at lightening the airships by the elimination of all unnecessary weight and included the removal of the dynamos, buffer wheels and bomb frames. Many other small items not considered essential were either taken out or replaced with lighter equipment. The folding tables which had been intended for the keel cabin were never installed, and the original plan of fitting a two-pounder gun on the top platform was also discarded. The rear car was replaced by a smaller and lighter one containing an engine with direct drive to a single two-bladed propeller 13 feet 6 inches in diameter. As there was now no space for the auxiliary controls, these were transferred to the keel cabin.

Some of these modifications had already been carried out on the first three ships, while others followed in due course. Together they effected a marked, if not substantial, improvement to the airships' performance.

No 24 required more than minor modifications, since she was so much heavier than the other ships. Close examination had failed to find any certain reason for this discrepancy and it had finally been attributed to Beardmore's having used rivets, fastenings and bracing pieces slightly larger and heavier than those of the other two firms. As their shed was needed immediately for the building of R.34 it was necessary to move the ship to her new station at East Fortune as soon as possible. This required extra lift to enable her to fly safely over the hilly countryside of southern Scotland, so in addition to the changes already made the drastic step was taken of removing all the machinery from the after car—engine, propeller, radiator and silencers. All these modifications brought the disposable lift up to nearly 6½ tons, but the price paid was a top speed barely in excess of 35 mph. In this form No 24 was delivered in October, 1917.

No 25 was delivered in the same month, but R.26, on which Vickers could not begin work until No 9 had left Barrow, arrived much later. All the recommended modifications were incorporated in the course of her construction. Although built more quickly than the others, in only about a year, she did not fly until March, 1918.

All four of the 23 class airships were flown extensively, but although rather more efficient than No 9 they still did not provide the performance which had been hoped for. No 23 herself had been commissioned on 15th October, 1917, and left on that day for Pulham. She had a top speed of 52 mph and flew a total of 8,426 miles in 321 hours 30 minutes. Although she carried out some patrols, usually under the command of Captain I. C. Little, she was used mainly for training and experimental work.

Trials were undertaken in January, 1918, at Pulham with a two-pounder

The two-pounder gun in its mounting on the top platform of No 23 during the trials at Pulham in January, 1917. The gas valves were placed on either side of the hull rather than at the top to avoid the risk of escaping gas being ignited during firing. *Fleet Air Arm Museum*

gun mounted on the top platform, as originally envisaged by the designers. Six shells were fired with the gun pointing downwards, but instead of embedding themselves in the mud of the airfield, as expected, they seem to have ricochetted through the surrounding countryside. The airship took the strain well, although some flexibility was present, which would have adversely affected aiming under combat conditions. No further action was taken in the matter because of the ever-present weight problem.

Later in 1918 No 23 was involved in another experiment, this time to determine whether an aeroplane could be carried by an airship and released in mid-air either to repel attackers or to take offensive action on its own account. A Sopwith Camel was suspended beneath the envelope by specially prepared fittings. For the first trial a dummy was placed in the cockpit and the controls were locked. As the airship flew over Pulham air station the aeroplane was released; it glided to the ground, showing that the slipping gear operated correctly. Another Camel was then taken up, this time piloted by Lieutenant R. E. Keys. As the aeroplane left No 23 the pilot had no trouble in starting the engine; he pulled out of the dive to fly around the airship before landing safely.

No 23 is walked across the field at Pulham towards the Sopwith Camel which is to be used in flying trials.   *Stuart Leslie collection*

No provision had been made for retrieval during flight, as the intention was that the aeroplane should make its own return to base after being in action. As with other unusual projects tried out during the war, nothing further was attempted. However, similar trials were held after the war with R.33, and the method was eventually perfected by the Americans in the early nineteen-thirties.

A noteworthy departure from routine training and testing befell No 23 on 6th December, 1917, when she was sent to make an unannounced daylight flight over London, arriving out of the mist from Pulham around midday. At a low altitude she circled over Buckingham Palace, Whitehall and the City, where thousands of Londoners clearly saw the lights twinkling in her gondolas, the red, white and blue roundels on her envelope and her designation numerals. Wartime censorship allowed press reports of the incident ("At last . . . a British Zeppelin"), but the airship's number could not be published, despite its having been so publicly displayed! Twice in the following year No 23 flew again over London, on one occasion accompanied by R.26, but these appear to have been the high points in an otherwise mundane and unwarlike career. She was deleted in September, 1919.

Her sister ship No 24 had a similar history, flying a total of 164 hours 40 minutes and covering 4,200 miles, but as the original intention of replacing her missing engine in a new and lighter car was never carried out she remained very slow. On one typical occasion, encountering an unexpectedly strong adverse wind near the Bass Rock, she remained for some time stationary, quite unable to make any headway. Despite this severe handicap she was used for training and convoy duties when conditions were deemed suitable, although she appears to have seen no action. She made her last wartime flight in June, 1918, but was retained in service and two months later had her bows strengthened to adapt her for mooring trials at Pulham, where Vickers were building a new type of high mast. The tests, which were carried out with both midship engines removed, were quite successful but were not completed finally until November, 1919. The following month No 24 was deleted and scrapped.

No 25 had been assembled slightly differently from the other three ships and always suffered from gasbag surging, which caused instability by moving the centre of lift unpredictably. In spite of this she flew 221 hours 5 minutes in service, covering 5,909 miles. Stationed for most of her career at Cranwell, she was used mainly for training before being deleted in September, 1919.

The last of the class was R.26. (The Admiralty decided on 18th December, 1917, that all future rigid airships should have the prefix R before their

No 23 carrying a Sopwith Camel during experiments at Pulham in 1918. The aeroplane was released successfully, but it could not be retrieved during flight. *Fleet Air Arm Museum*

number.) Apparently the only one of her class to incorporate all the design changes, she was commissioned on 22nd April, 1918, and stationed at Howden. During tests she was found to have a disposable lift of 6¼ tons, a top speed of 54 mph and a ceiling of 3,500 feet. It was also discovered that if the engines were stopped at 53 mph the speed fell to 18 mph in two minutes, so great was the drag.

By the end of the year she had flown 191 hours 29 minutes, of which the highlights were a flight with No 23 over London on 25th October and a patrol of 40 hours 40 minutes on 4th/5th June, when she was commanded by Major T.

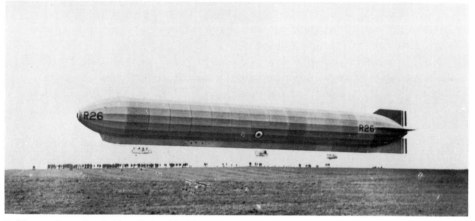

R.26 was the only airship of the 23 Class to incorporate all the recommended design changes intended to save weight. She flew 198 hours in service, the same as No 9.

Royal Aeronautical Society

Elmsley. This was the longest flight yet by a British rigid, beating No 23's previous record, set up a few days earlier, by 32 minutes.

Later in the year she was transferred to Pulham and, commanded by Major Watt, she supervised the surrender of German submarines at Harwich on 20th November, 1918. In January, 1919, R.26 flew a further 6 hours 18 minutes, and then had her bows specially strengthened before being experimentally moored out in the open, using the "three wire system". Despite a tendency to assume a tail up attitude—overcome by fastening sandbags to the after guys—she survived for over a week without harm. Then the weather worsened, rain soaked her envelope and a snowstorm finally beat her into the ground. Her cars were removed, allowing her to float again, but it was soon found that the damage she had sustained was too severe for repairs to be worthwhile. On 24th February the order was given for her to be scrapped and her official deletion followed on 10th March.

CHAPTER FIFTEEN

The 23X Class

THE 23X class was a development of the 23 class, itself merely an improvement to the No 9 design. Four of the class were originally planned, with numbers running consecutively from R.27 to R.30, but the lessons learned from the L-33 episode caused R.28 and R.30 to be cancelled in order to concentrate resources on the new R.33 class.

R.27 and R.29 differed from their predecessors in that minor modifications to the shape of the hull had given them slightly more gas capacity, but more importantly in the elimination of the external keel corridor. The function of this feature was primarily to distribute the weight of fuel tanks, ballast bags and similar items, and only secondarily to strengthen the hull, so its absence in the two 23X ships was intended to effect a considerable saving of weight without causing any significant loss of strength and also to improve manoeuvrability.

The various loads were concentrated at the bulkheads and suspended from the radial wiring which maintained the hull in its correct polygonal shape. An internal corridor which allowed the crew to travel between the cars was formed by inverted U-shaped ribs positioned above the two lowest longitudinal girders, the surrounding gasbags being appropriately shaped. The corridor also gave access to the ballast bags and petrol tanks. The latter were interconnected by a long, wide aluminium tube running underneath them, an arrangement which helped with refuelling and could be used in an emergency to jettison fuel.

The four engines were again Rolls Royce Eagle V12 designs, but they were the later Series 6 models, which produced 300 hp at full revolutions. The engine arrangement was the same as that used originally for the 23 class ships, with pairs of swivelling propellers in the forward and after gondolas and twin engines driving fixed propellers in the midship car.

The radical and original decision to do without a normal keel was fully vindicated when the first trials were held. Not only were the two airships able to turn more quickly than their forerunners but the real benefit was found when the lift and trim tests were held; the disposable lift was more than 8½ tons, much better than any previous British airship and allowing a more effective bomb load to be carried as well as sufficient fuel for extended cruising. One handicap common to both ships, as well as to their predecessors, was the absorbent nature of the hull's outer covering of doped linen; a few hours of rain could add around a ton of water to the weight.

R.27 was commissioned on 29th June, 1918, and flew 89 hours 40 minutes in

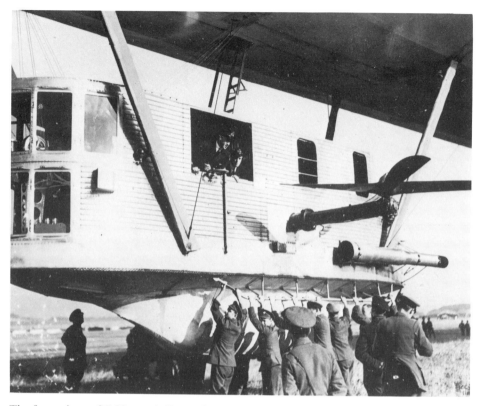

The forward car of R.29 was similar to that of No 9, but the swivelling propellers were mounted lower on the car. A ladder connected the control car to the keel.   *Fleet Air Arm Museum*

service, commanded by Major Ommaney, before coming to a disastrous end. On 16th August she was in the hangar at Howden at the same time that some riggers were helpfully trying to make a new airship by attaching a spare SS Zero car to a disused envelope. While they were completing the job some petrol was spilt into the car; it was not mopped up. The spilt petrol was ignited a little later by a spark when an unsuspecting operator came to test the W/T equipment. The flames, fed by both fuel and gas, expanded within seconds into a conflagration that totally destroyed not only the makeshift blimp and R.27 but also SSZ.38 and SSZ.54, which had been moored nearby. The hangar itself survived, although badly damaged. One airman who failed to get out in time lost his life.

R.29 was a more fortunate craft in every way, and was the only British rigid airship actually to meet the enemy in combat. She was commissioned on 20th

June, 1918, based at East Fortune and in a brief operational career of less than five months flew 335 hours and covered an estimated 8,215 miles. Once she carried out a patrol of over 30 hours, twice more she made a flight longer than 20 hours and three times she encountered German U-boats. The first escaped, the second ran on to a mine and only the last was attacked.

On Sunday, 29th September, at about half past one in the afternoon and in exceptionally calm conditions R.29, captained by Major G. M. Thomas, was escorting a convoy bound for Scandinavia when a faint patch of oil was seen discolouring the water near Newbiggin Point. A message, "Oil patch rising below me," was flashed by Aldis lamp to HMS *Ouse*, one of the escorting destroyers, which turned at once to help. Her captain could not see the slight evidence that was apparent to the airmen high overhead and he signalled for more information, "Drop light over it." In reply the airship indicated the probable whereabouts of the submarine by dropping not a flare but a 230 lb bomb, the destroyer joining in the attack with two depth charges as the first explosion subsided.

Then R.29 dropped a second bomb and a calcium flare to mark the position of the oil patch, at which another destroyer, HMS *Star*, joined with *Ouse* and two armed trawlers to add more depth charges to the barrage. At half past two HMS *Star* reported considerable quantities of oil rising to the surface, and the

Seen here in her original form, R.29 was undoubtedly the most successful of the eight British wartime rigid airships. She flew 351 hours in this form. *Royal Aeronautical Society*

destroyers then steamed off after the convoy. A buoy was placed as a marker by one of the trawlers and a deep depth charge was dropped, while R.29 remained on watch for more than an hour. When she at last left to rejoin the convoy at four o'clock large amounts of oil were still bubbling to the surface.

It was subsequently confirmed from Intelligence reports that *UB.115* had been destroyed in the attack. It was the sole success recorded by any British wartime rigid.

After the Armistice R.29 flew another 16 hours before May, 1919, when her midship car was replaced by a smaller and lighter type containing only one engine driving a single propeller. In this modified form she flew a further 87 hours, including a flight in June over Edinburgh, Berwick, May Island and the Firth of Forth, when she was accompanied by R.34. She was finally deleted in October, 1919, having covered an estimated 11,334 miles in service, more than any other British rigid up to that time.

R.29 was fitted with a smaller and lighter midship car in May, 1919. In this photograph she is seen at East Fortune during experiments on fabrics and dopes, various sections of her hull having been given different treatments. *Scottish Museum of Flight*

CHAPTER SIXTEEN

The R.31 Class

INITIALLY the development work on British rigid airships came from the Vickers design team led by H. B. Pratt and Barnes Wallis, and it was they who were responsible for nearly all the rigid airships flown in Britain before the Armistice. The exceptions were provided by Short Bros, who were accepted as suitable constructors but who received directions from the Admiralty, where a new team led by Constructor-Commander C. I. R. Campbell had been set up.

This body aimed at first to direct designs to their own requirements and eventually to oversee construction as well by establishing a Royal Airship Works. The second aim was achieved only later, but the Admiralty team was soon able to dictate to various firms and the airships that eventually flew from Short Bros' new shed at Cardington were largely the team's product.

The design itself was largely based on that pioneered by the German firm of Schutte-Lanz, the secrets of which are said to have been smuggled to Britain by a Swiss, one Müller, a foreman in the girder shop at the Schutte-Lanz plant at Mannheim-Rheinau, and sold to the Admiralty. In Britain the design was unique, for the central feature was a framework not of the usual duralumin but of wood. Two airships were eventually constructed to the same design, both at Cardington. The first of these, R.31, was a wartime ship, if only just.

She was much larger than any previous British airship, being 615 feet in length, nearly as long as a Dreadnought battleship, and with a diameter of 65 feet 6 inches. She contained nineteen gasbags, giving a total capacity of 1,500,000 cubic feet, a gross lift of 46 tons and a disposable lift of 16½ tons, far greater than any earlier airship built in Britain. Her wooden girders, made of spruce-stiffened three-ply, had the cross section of a ten-inch equilateral triangle and were assembled with cold water casein cement before being reinforced with hardwood blocks and mild steel gusset plates. Linen was wrapped round areas of stress, and after assembly each girder was braced with diagonal wires and each transverse ring with both diametral and chordal wires. These were all solid piano wire and, together with the gas cell retaining wires, measured some hundred miles in total length.

Apart from the wooden construction, the two other advanced features which distinguished her from other British rigids were the streamlined stern and a control car fitted flush to the hull. This was practicable as the car contained no engine, contrary to previous practice. Instead, each of the six 300 hp Rolls Royce Eagle engines was installed in its own car, suspended in pairs further aft along the underside of the hull. The engine cars were streamlined, although their sleek contours were marred by fixed radiators, the action of which was regulated by shutters. The engines in the two midship cars could operate their propellers in reverse as an aid to manoeuvring or braking.

An internal triangular-section keel corridor provided a means of communication between the control car and the engine cars, as well as being the conventional depository for fuel tanks, water ballast bags, bombs and other items. The wooden structure allowed considerable flexibility; one disconcerting feature of the design was that two men standing at opposite ends of this keel corridor lost sight of each other when the airship turned and the girders flexed.

R.31 made her first flight in August, 1918, piloted by Squadron Commander W. C. Hicks. Her top speed proved to be an unexpected 70 mph, much the fastest achieved in this country up to that time. As a result it was decided to

The R.31 is prepared for her first flight from Cardington in August, 1918. As built she had six engines, each in its own separate car, and the control room was attached close to the hull.

Royal Aeronautical Society

R.31 in flight after she had been deprived of one of the after engines. She became slightly slower, but her disposable lift was greatly increased. *Fleet Air Arm Museum*

reduce the number of engines to five by replacing a pair of cars with a single car positioned centrally, so saving some three tons of weight.

A second trial in October showed that the top speed had been reduced only slightly, to about 65 mph, and that in other respects also the ship was extremely promising, although the controls were found to be somewhat too powerful in operation. Towards the end of the flight, however, disaster was narrowly avoided in an accident probably not unconnected with the ship's peculiar construction. The top vertical fin acted as a kingpost to support the horizontal fins, and as the downward air pressure on these became excessive the girder in the vertical fin suddenly broke under the strain.

Commander Hicks immediately dropped ballast from the bows, raising the nose so that the pressure was reversed and the horizontal fins held in position while the airship kept moving. As the operation of the elevators and rudders was hampered by trailing fabric the riggers had to climb out on to the top of the hull to clear away the wreckage. Their efforts were successful and the airship remained steady and was able to return in safety to Cardington, although as soon as the engines were stopped the horizontal fins collapsed, deprived of the support provided by air pressure.

The whole tail assembly was repaired and reduced in size, while the upper fin was suitably strengthened. At the same time the streamlined tail cone was removed and replaced by a gun platform with a wide arc of fire. These modifications were quickly completed, and without further trials R.31 was commissioned on 6th November, leaving Cardington on that day for East Fortune. On the way, presumably because there were signs of stress damage to some of the girders, she called in at Howden, from where she resumed her journey six days later, on the morrow of the Armistice. Almost immediately, it would seem, there appeared further damage, so she returned to Howden and was housed in the hangar which had been so badly damaged when R.27 was destroyed a short while before.

There she remained for several months. Dampness and neglect caused her glue to soften and her framework to disintegrate beyond the possibility of repair, and the following February work began on dismantling her.

R.31 was not, however, officially deleted until July. Her total service flying time was only 4 hours 55 minutes, but she could have been a very successful ship if the circumstances and the constructional expertise had been rather different. It is said that the wood from the framework was purchased by a local dealer who attempted to sell it for kindling, not realizing until too late that it had been fireproofed.

The other ship in this class, R.32, was not completed until 1919 and was therefore not a wartime craft. A popular aircraft, she flew over 200 hours, mainly training American airmen, before being dismantled in early 1921.

CHAPTER SEVENTEEN

On the Ground

AIRSHIPS spent but a small part of their lives in the air, and for every man who flew there were perhaps a score who never left the ground but whose work was just as vital. However, in the First World War airships were much less labour intensive than aeroplanes, despite their more complicated handling requirements, and it has been calculated that for every hour flown by airships 1.62 men had to be employed; for aeroplanes, the corresponding figure was 3.52.

At the Armistice there were 7,114 officers and men in the Airship Service, of whom the great majority never flew but were concerned with maintenance, repairs, administration, catering or other mundane but essential matters. And just as the aircrews could not fly without the support of a numerous ground crew, so the airships themselves needed time, work and attention while they were on the ground.

Unlike an aeroplane, which could be left unattended in any small shed, an airship required both a large hangar and regular attention. Most of the British non-rigid airships had envelopes made of two layers of cotton fabric with a proofing of rubber between and a second proofing on the inner surface. The exterior was at first doped, frequently with a yellowish colour, but after about 1917 it was usually finished off with a deposit of aluminium on unvulcanized rubber in order to reflect the sunlight and so reduce superheating. It was at about the same time that the practice began of displaying the airship's designation letters and numerals on each side of the envelope. Previously these had been either painted on the car or not shown at all.

Rigid airships used linen for the outer envelope and normally displayed their designation letter and numeral at both bow and stern on each side. The internal gasbags were of cotton fabric lined with goldbeater's skin. Since filling with gas was a lengthy process it was neither practicable nor desirable to empty airships after every flight and they normally remained fully inflated.

However, even without rents or punctures, there was inevitably some degree of porosity in the gasbag which meant that gas had to be constantly added, the exact amount depending on several factors, including the age of the material, which deteriorated rapidly in service. Not only did gas leak continuously from envelopes and gasbags but air also seeped inwards, gradually contaminating the lifting medium, reducing the buoyancy and creating a

Gas bottles being unloaded from a railway waggon at an operational airship station. In the background is a small shed for a non-rigid airship, with its windscreen just visible on the right.

Norman Peake

potentially explosive mixture. After several months of service, therefore, it became necessary for the ground crew to deflate an airship completely and to reinflate with fresh gas. Each airship station had its own plant to produce hydrogen, which was stored in cylinders under high pressure until required. The operation of these gas plants could be a risky business; two men were killed by a violent explosion at Pulham in April, 1917.

A close watch had to be kept for leaks, of course, and, with the airships tethered down safely in the hangar, riggers would climb over the great bulk of their charges with patches, rubber solution and dope for repairs. It was customary for men engaged in this task to whistle or sing as they worked, although not for idle reasons. Any change towards shrillness in the sound was an audible warning of the presence of leaked hydrogen, which could be dangerous to the health of the riggers as well as to the airship. As an additional safety measure they usually carried knives at their belts, since it was not unknown for a man to fall through the material right into the gasbag; he had then only moments in which to cut himself free. Although hydrogen is both odourless and tasteless and is not of itself poisonous, it has unpleasant effects when inhaled in quantity and can cause asphyxiation. One man was overcome on No 9 while checking for leaks and was badly injured when he dropped to the ground unconscious. Another fell into the gasbag of SSZ.55 and slashed his way out through both ballonet and envelope only just in time to avoid suffocation.

Occasionally it became necessary to check the inner surface of the gasbag material, or the internal suspensions which were a feature of the Astra Torres designs, while the envelope was fully inflated. This involved using breathing apparatus called "proto gear"; originally developed for mine rescue, it consisted of a chemical-filled bag into which the operator breathed, a spring clip for his nose and two cylinders of oxygen strapped to his back. He made his entry by way of the six-foot-long tube—known as a "petticoat"—which connected the valve to the envelope. This was normally tucked away inside the envelope, but for access it was pulled down and tied at the upper end, so allowing the valve to be removed and the bottom end of the tube to be placed on the top rungs of a

An aerial view of the gas-producing plant on a wartime airship station. In this plant hydrogen was made by mixing ferro silicon with a solution of caustic soda. *Norman Peake*

ladder. The operator climbed up inside the tube, which was fastened below him. Then the top lashing was untied, allowing him to enter the envelope without loss of gas pressure. To get out, the process was reversed. This apparatus was not normally kept at operational air stations but was used at Kingsnorth, Barrow and Wormwood Scrubs, where the airships were assembled and major repairs undertaken.

While the riggers attended to envelopes, cables and other connected matters, the engineers serviced the various types of engine with which the airships were fitted. Those used in airships were required to have very different characteristics from those used in aeroplanes, for while the latter had to produce high performance over a short period the former needed to be flexible, reliable over long periods and yet capable of being repaired during flight.

The powerful but complex and inflexible rotary engines which were fitted to many fighter aircraft of the period were totally unsuited to airships and were not used. Instead a wide variety of engines, both British and foreign, were employed and frequently interchanged as circumstances dictated. All types lacked the reliability and efficiency of later engines; they consumed oil in large quantities, and only by constant attention were they prevented from breaking down even more frequently than actually happened. Indeed, those men attending the early SS ships usually started the engines, even in the hangar, by standing on a skid and swinging the propeller from behind by hand; this was regarded as good practice for the frequent occasions when it was necessary to carry out running repairs during flight. Problems with the air-cooled engines were often caused by faulty cylinder heads, which cracked so often in the SS ships that it was not unknown for more than one to be changed during a single patrol. And this despite every care being taken on the ground to service and check each item thoroughly.

One of the most persistent problems facing the Airship Service was the housing of all their charges. To manoeuvre a large airship into a hangar only a little higher or wider than the dirigible herself was difficult at any time, and in windy conditions often impossible. To leave the ship out in the open in these circumstances was to invite certain disaster, however, and the crew's only recourse then was to rip the envelope, so releasing all the gas at once and allowing the envelope to be packed for subsequent repair.

In an attempt to avoid this drastic measure—which could not, in any event, be applied to rigids—many experiments were carried out to find alternative methods of housing or securing airships. One fascinating proposal, made by Sir Robert MacAlpine, was to dig enormous tunnels into convenient hillsides, so creating safe shelters which could easily be enlarged as required. Neither this nor a similar proposal to use dry docks temporarily roofed over was ever implemented, however. Several trials were made of high mooring masts, to the top of which the bow of the airship was fastened in such a way that she swung

Above: An air mechanic prepares to swing the propeller as the Coastal airship C.9 is made ready for flight at Mullion. *Fleet Air Arm Museum*

Below: R.33 at the Pulham mooring mast in 1921. Many experiments were made in an attempt to find an alternative to the enormous hangars which were necessary to house the large rigid airships. *Imperial War Museum*

like a weathervane, always into the wind. There was also the "three wire system", pioneered at Pulham by No 9 and intended mainly to be used in emergencies;

When rigid airships were built the gasbags were inserted into the frame during construction and partly inflated. This is R.34 at the Beardmore factory at Inchinnan, Glasgow, in late 1918.
Flight International

this involved leading three cables from widely separated anchorages to a point beneath the bows of the airship, whose lift then kept the pyramid taut. Yet another system was the use of a drogue or sea anchor which allowed an airship to be moored at sea.

None of these solutions proved wholly satisfactory and huge hangars had to be built, in spite of the expense, wherever airfields were required. The doors of these "sheds", as they were usually called, were much too heavy to be opened manually; some form of tractor, often by the end of the war an obsolete tank, was usually brought in to provide the requisite power. As a protection against crosswinds enormous sidescreens were sometimes erected in conjunction with the hangars, but these created eddies which added to the problems of manoeuvring airships in bad weather.

The great cost of these hangars was a contributory reason for the slow development of the rigid airship. The Vickers constructional shed at Barrow at 535 feet was only some three yards longer than airship No 9. It was planned at one time to build a new shed with a length of 900 feet, but this never came about and the Vickers designers were perforce restricted in their ambitions. The best ship they ever made was R.80, but her length was limited to 530 feet, which prevented her from attaining the efficiency that greater size would have given. Armstrong Whitworth, of Selby in Yorkshire, Beardmore's, of Inchinnan, near Glasgow, and Short Bros, of Cardington, were eventually able to erect sheds 700 feet long, and it was these that enabled them to build R.33, R.34 and R.31 respectively, each well over 600 feet in length. In addition to these and other constructional sheds, of course, there was the complementary need for operational sheds of a similar size. By the end of the war, double sheds had been erected at East Fortune, Pulham and Howden, at an approximate cost of £150,000 each, and smaller ones were numerous.

However, the greatest challenge facing those trying to build up Britain's airship fleet was surely that of providing the airships themselves, in large numbers and without delays. In this task the administrators, constructors and assemblers succeeded admirably, despite the comparative failure of the rigid airship programme. When war broke out only seven airships were in service, but during the four years of conflict their number increased thirtyfold.

Manpower was in short supply, skilled workers were few, the constructional techniques were unfamiliar and experience was lacking; nevertheless, the achievement was considerable.

The No 2 shed at Pulham cost £150,000 to erect and could house two large rigids. R.33 and R.34, each 643 feet long, 79 feet in diameter and 92 feet in overall height, were moored in the shed side by side in July, 1919. *Fleet Air Arm Museum*

CHAPTER EIGHTEEN

Conclusion

THE SIGNING of the Armistice on 11th November, 1918, brought an immediate halt to a conflict that only a few weeks earlier had appeared to have no end in sight. Although the Armistice was theoretically no more than a truce while a final peace treaty was negotiated, it was recognized by all combatants that the war could never be resumed and the effect was almost instant. For a few days airship patrols continued in case there were submarines whose commanders did not yet know hostilities had ceased, and the search for mines continued for a while, but that was all.

The story of British airships in the years after the war is in general one of decline and disappointment. On 11th November, 1918, there were 107 airships in service, of which six were rigids. During the next few months six more non-rigids, NS.16, SSZ.71, SSZ.76, SSZ.77, SST.14 and SSE.3, were delivered, but they were the last. The rigid airships in course of construction, R.32, R.33 and

Left: In the control cabin of R.34 during the transatlantic flight in 1919. In the centre is the elevator coxswain, with the steering coxswain on the left.

Opposite page: Women workers join their male colleagues on the handling ropes as R.34 is taken from Beardmore's works at Inchinnan in March, 1919.
Royal Aeronautical Society

R.34, were soon completed and delivered to the Admiralty, but the great plans for a fleet of British rigid airships were progressively scaled down until only two more were completed, R.36 and R.80. There was also R.38, but she was to be sold to America immediately upon completion.

Many of the wartime airships never flew again after the Armistice; they were soon deflated and packed up to await the inevitable decision. Several continued flight training, largely for the benefit of the Americans waiting to take over R.38, but peacetime flying was in general greatly reduced.

In July, 1919, there came the greatest achievement by a British airship in peacetime when R.34 flew from East Fortune to New York in 108 hours 12 minutes and then returned to Pulham in 75 hours 3 minutes. The first was a world endurance record, beating that set up a few months earlier by NS.11, and was the first east to west crossing of the Atlantic by any aircraft. At the same time R.34 also accomplished the first double crossing and a non-stop flight between the United Kingdom and the United States which was not only the first ever but the last for another fourteen years. She was captained on this epoch-making flight by Major G. H. Scott and carried Edward Maitland as a passenger, as well as a cat and a stowaway.

By this time, however, many of the airships which had survived the war had already been scrapped in the interests of economy. Indeed, the seeds of this run-down had been sown much earlier, on 1st April, 1918, when the RNAS had

ceased to exist and its personnel had joined with the men of the RFC to form the Royal Air Force. To the men flying in airships this had meant little real change at first, since even their new uniforms did not arrive for many months and it was long after the end of the war that the airships themselves were handed over to the RAF. Until then the Admiralty retained control of all airships and their deployment, despite being no longer responsible for the men who flew them. The new arrangements had also meant other anomalies, such as Army style ranks to begin with, but the duties of both airships and airshipmen remained until the end of the war as they had been before reorganization.

The senior airship officer in Britain was Brigadier General Edward

Air Commodore Edward Maitland was the greatly admired leader of the Airship Service during the latter part of the war. He was among those who died in the wreck of the R.38 in 1921. *Royal Aeronautical Society*

Maitland, who had transferred to the RAF after a year as Supervisor of Airships at the Admiralty, but how far he agreed with the policies of the new Air Ministry it is impossible to know. Nevertheless, his energy and enthusiasm had done much to ensure the efficiency and high morale of the Airship Service during the latter part of the war, regardless of paymaster or employer, and he had ambitious plans for peacetime airships.

His superior, Sir Hugh Trenchard, the head of the RAF, had neither experience of airships nor any enthusiasm for them, and the other former members of the RFC who dominated the Air Ministry were equally determined to concentrate the restricted funds of peacetime military aviation on aeroplanes. In October, 1919, when the RAF took over the airships from the Admiralty, there was a mass deletion of more than sixty, leaving only a handful still in existence for training purposes. By late 1920 the only non-rigids remaining in commission were NS.7 and SSE.3. It seems that the former made her last flight on 25th October, 1920, and the latter three days later. Both ships were deleted the following year when the Airship Service was finally closed down as a separate entity by the Air Ministry.

In August, 1921, came the disaster of R.38, which broke up in mid-air, killing forty-four of the forty-nine men on board, among whom were Edward Maitland, R. S. Montagu, C. I. R. Campbell, I. C. Little, G. M. Thomas and other stalwart proponents of the airship. The tragic loss of these men, no less than the destruction of the airship, ensured that there would be no return to the use of military dirigibles in this country.

The R.34 had been wrecked the previous January, R.32 had just been dismantled and R.80 was scrapped within weeks. Although both R.33 and R.36 survived for some years more they were retained only as a token, and their eventual deletion was inevitable. The armed services of other countries, notably those of France and America, continued to use airships successfully for many years, but no airships were ever again employed by either the RAF or the Royal Navy, for the last of all British rigid dirigibles, R.100 and R.101, were both civilian aircraft.

From the first flight of *Nulli Secundus* to the scrapping of R.33 in 1928 was a mere score of years, but if British airships had only an hour upon the stage, it was still a crowded hour of glorious strife. For the short span of the First World War, as never before or since, these rather primitive aircraft, flown by a few brave men, held the key to Britain's survival.

The beautiful lines of the German L-32, the third of the class on which British technicians based the design of R.33 and R.34, are apparent in this photograph.   *Deutsches Museum, Munich*

Britain and Germany both employed dirigibles in large numbers, but the airships themselves and the manner of their deployment were in striking contrast. The German airships were nearly all large, sophisticated and expensive, while the British craft were nearly all small, simple and cheap. The German ships were used in general very unwisely, inflicting relatively unimportant damage on Britain in bombing raids at a terrible cost in destruction of their own machines and men. Sixteen of the German Navy's airships were destroyed by fire with the loss of all hands due to British aircraft or guns, and several others perished only slightly less tragically.

The British airships, by comparison, were used carefully and sensibly. Even if the building programme, with its wasteful use of money and resources to produce inefficient and expensive rigid airships, is criticized, yet all the airships once built were deployed with the greatest skill, being concentrated on the role at which they excelled and preventing the enemy from winning the long battle at sea. No British ships were wasted on suicidal bombing missions over land; whereas although the Zeppelins carried out some scouting work for the German Navy, their great potential for long-range action over the sea in support of the U-boats, by searching out convoys and destroying British airships, was never realized or even explored.

It is surely both significant and ironic that there was seemingly not a single occasion during the war when airships from the two countries met in a direct conflict that could only have been very uneven, given the undeniable superiority of the German Zeppelins in both performance and firepower. The prospect was certainly envisaged in Britain, for the larger guns which were tried out experimentally on some airships were intended mainly as a defence against possible Zeppelin attacks.

The last operational appearance of the British wartime airships was at a symbolic time and occasion. When the German fleet came in to surrender in late November, 1918, they were met out in the North Sea by British warships and escorted into the Firth of Forth. It was a time of high drama and patriotic fervour when many sailors claimed to have heard Drake's drum beating as the grey columns of German warships steamed slowly towards Rosyth, led by the light cruiser HMS *Cardiff*. Flying on the starboard bow was NS.7, while mounting guard above the centre of the fleet was NS.8. At about the same time, much further south, the German submarines were surrendering at Harwich, while above their heads hovered the ceremonial threat of R.26 and SR.1. The presence of these four airships, representing all their comrades, was both deserved and appropriate; without them, the narrow victory could well have been a close defeat.

Technical Details of British Wartime Airships

No 2 (Willows)

Envelope capacity ....35,000 cubic feet
Engine ....35 hp Anzani
Gross lift ....1.1 tons
Endurance ....3 hours
Top speed ....25 mph

No 3 (Astra Torres)

Envelope capacity ....230,000 cubic feet
Length ....248 feet
Engines ....Two 200 hp Chenu
Gross lift ....6.8 tons
Top speed ....51 mph

No 4 (Parseval)

Envelope capacity ....310,000 cubic feet
Length ....276 feet
Engines ....Two 180 hp Maybach
Gross lift ....9.3 tons
Top speed ....42 mph

No 17 (Beta)

Envelope capacity ....42,000 cubic feet
Length ....108 feet
Engine ....50 hp Clerget
Gross lift ....1.3 tons
Top speed ....35 mph

No 18 (Gamma)

Envelope capacity ....101,000 cubic feet
Engines ....Two 45 hp Iris
Gross lift ....3 tons
Top speed ....30 mph

No 19 (Delta)

Envelope capacity ....175,000 cubic feet
Engines ....Two 110 hp White & Poppe
Gross lift..5.2 tons
Top speed..42 mph

No 20 (Eta)

Envelope capacity.......................................118,000 cubic feet
Engines ....Two 80 hp Canton-Unne
Gross lift..3.5 tons
Top speed..42 mph

SS Airships (B.E.2c car)

Envelope capacity ....60,000 cubic feet
Ballonets (two) capacity ....12,750 cubic feet
Length ....143 feet 5 inches
Diameter...27 feet 9 inches
Height..43 feet 5 inches
Plane area (each)..110 square feet
Car length..24 feet
Engine..70 or 75 hp Renault
Propeller...Four-bladed, 9 feet diameter
Petrol tanks (three) capacity ....59½ gallons total
Water ballast capacity..................................19 gallons
Gross lift ....1.85 tons
Disposable lift (for crew,
fuel, armament, ballast, etc.) ....0.64 tons
Endurance at full speed ....7–8 hours
Endurance at half throttle ....14–16 hours
Top speed..50 mph (52 with three planes)
Climb ....700 feet per minute
Turning circle..32 seconds minimum

SS Airships (Maurice Farman cars)

As above except:
Envelope capacity.......................................60,000 or 70,000 cubic feet
Ballonets (two) capacity ....12,750 or 19,600 cubic feet
Diameter...30 or 32 feet
Car length..20 feet
Engine..75 hp Renault air-cooled
Petrol tank capacity ....64 gallons
Water ballast capacity..................................26 gallons
Gross lift (larger envelope)............................2.2 tons
Disposable lift (smaller envelope) ....0.6 tons

Disposable lift (larger envelope).....................0.8 tons (approx.)
Top speed...40 mph
Climb ....790 feet per minute
Turning circle...47 seconds minimum, 180 yards diameter

SS Airships (Armstrong Whitworth cars)

As above except:
Envelope capacity ....70,000 cubic feet
Ballonets (two) capacity ....19,600 cubic feet
Diameter...32 feet
Car length..26 feet
Engine..100 hp water-cooled Green
Petrol tanks (three) capacity ....90 gallons total
Water ballast capacity.................................30 gallons
Gross lift...2.2 tons
Disposable lift..0.7 tons
Endurance (at full speed) ....12 hours
Endurance (at half speed)............................24 hours
Top speed...45 mph
Climb ....500 feet per minute
Turning circle.......................................43 seconds minimum

An unusual view of the Armstrong Whitworth car of SS.41, showing the four-bladed propeller and the air scoop supplying air to the ballonets. *Norman Peake*

SSP Airships

As above except:
Envelope capacity ....70,000 cubic feet
Diameter..30 feet
Ballonets (two) capacity ....19,600 cubic feet
Petrol tanks (two) capacity ....102 gallons total
Engine..75 hp Rolls Royce or 100 hp Green
Gross lift..2.2 tons
Top speed..52 mph

SSZ Airships

As above except:
Envelope capacity ....70,000 cubic feet
Diameter...30 feet
Height ....46 feet

SST.2 was based at Kingsnorth, Polegate and Mullion and flew 91 hours in service during her six months in commission. The twin air scoops, matching the twin engines, can be seen to the rear of the car. *Royal Aeronautical Society*

Ballonets (two) capacity ....19,600 cubic feet
Petrol tanks (two) capacity ....102 gallons total
Car, boat-shaped, streamlined, length............17 feet 6 inches
Water ballast capacity.................................26 gallons
Engine...75 hp water-cooled Rolls Royce
Gross lift...2.2 tons
Disposable lift ....0.6 tons
Endurance ....17 hours
Top speed...53 mph
Climb ....1,200 feet per minute
Turning circle.......................................40 seconds minimum, 230 yards diameter

SST Airships

As above except:
Envelope capacity ....100,000 cubic feet
Ballonets 4
Length ....165 feet
Diameter..35 feet 6 inches
Height..49 feet
Car ....Streamlined and waterproofed
Engines ....Two 100 hp Sunbeam or two 75 hp Rolls
Royce
Gross lift..3.1 tons
Disposable lift ....1.0 ton
Top speed...57 mph

Coastal Airships

Envelope capacity ....170,000 cubic feet
Length ....195 feet 6 inches
Diameter..37 feet
Height..52 feet 1 inch
Ballonets (four) capacity ....51,000 cubic feet
Car length..33 feet 9 inches
Engines ....Two 150 hp water-cooled Sunbeams.
Later, after Sunbeam replaced by 220 hp
Renault. Forward engine sometimes re-
placed by 100 hp Berliet or similar
Petrol tanks (two) capacity ....220 gallons total
Water ballast capacity................................85 gallons
Gross lift..4.94 tons
Disposable lift ....1.6 tons
Endurance (at full speed) ....11 hours
Endurance (at half speed)............................22 hours
Top speed...52 mph
Ceiling...8,000 feet
Climb ....1,000 feet per 40 seconds

C Star Airships

Envelope capacity ....210,000 cubic feet
Length ....207 feet (C*1–3); 217 feet (C*4–10)
Diameter..47 feet
Height ....56 feet
Ballonets (six) capacity ....68,860 cubic feet
Car length...33 feet
Engines ....Forward, 110 hp Berliet; after, 220 hp
                                        Renault or 240 hp Fiat
Main petrol tanks (four) capacity ....340 gallons total
Service petrol tanks (two) capacity................60 gallons
Water ballast capacity................................40 gallons
Gross lift ....6.46 tons
Disposable lift ....1.8 tons
Endurance (at full speed) ....10 hours
Endurance (at half speed)..........................20 hours
Top speed...57 mph
Ceiling ....9,500 feet
Climb ....1,000 feet per 1 min. 19 secs

North Sea Airships

Envelope capacity ....360,000 cubic feet
Length ....260 feet
Diameter...57 feet
Height ....69 feet
Ballonets (six) capacity ....128,000 cubic feet
Engines ....At first two 250 hp Rolls Royce Later two
                                        240 hp Fiat
Gross lift..10.85 tons
Disposable lift ....3.8 tons
Endurance ....24 hours
Top speed...57 mph

Parseval Airships (Vickers)

Envelope capacity ....364,000 cubic feet
Length ....301 feet
Diameter...51 feet
Height ....70 feet
Ballonets (two) capacity ....110,000 cubic feet
Engines ....Two 180 hp Maybach
Gross lift...11 tons
Top speed...43 mph

SR.1

Envelope capacity ....441,000 cubic feet
Length ....270 feet
Diameter..55 feet
Engines ....One 180 hp SPA (later removed), two 180 hp Itala
Gross lift...13.3 tons
Top speed..51 mph

No 9

Total gas capacity ....846,000 cubic feet
Overall length..526 feet
Diameter..53 feet
Height...76 feet
Gasbags ....Seventeen
Engines ....At first, four 180 hp Wolseley Maybach. Later, two 180 hp and one 240 hp Maybach
Gross lift...25.6 tons
Disposable lift ....3.8 tons
Top speed..43 mph

HMA No 9 emerges from her assembly shed at Barrow. To the right is the waterside structure in which the ill-fated HMA No 1 had been built five years earlier.   *H. G. Parker*

23 Class Airships

Total gas capacity ....942,000 cubic feet
Overall length ....535 feet
Diameter ....53 feet
Height ....75 feet
Gasbags ....Eighteen
Engines ....Four 250 hp Rolls Royce
Gross lift ....28.5 tons
Disposable lift ....6.5 tons
Top speed...52 mph

23X Class Airships

Total gas capacity ....990,000 cubic feet
Overall length ....539 feet
Diameter ....53 feet
Height ....75 feet
Gasbags ....Eighteen
Engines ....Four 300 hp Rolls Royce
Gross lift...30.1 tons
Disposable lift ....8.5 tons
Top speed...55 mph

31 Class Airships

Total gas capacity ....1,500,000 cubic feet
Overall length ....615 feet
Diameter ....65 feet 6 inches
Gasbags ....Nineteen
Engines ....At first, six 300 hp Rolls Royce Later, five
ditto
Gross lift...46 tons
Disposable lift ....At first, 16.5 tons. Later, 19.5 tons
Top speed...At first, 70 mph. Later, 65 mph

British Military Airships 1914–1921

Designation number	Delivery date	Deletion or transfer date	Reason	Hours flown	Details
No 2	1913	1915	Us.	—	Willows
No 3	1913	5.1916	Us.	—	Astra Torres
No 4	1913	17.7.17	Us.	—	Parseval
No 17	1912	5.1916	Us.	—	*Beta*, ex-Army
No 18	1910	5.1916	Us.	—	*Gamma*, ex-Army
No 19	1912	5.1916	Us.	—	*Delta*, ex-Army
No 20	1913	5.1916	Us.	—	*Eta*, ex-Army
No 8	1914	5.1916	Us.	—	Astra Torres
No 10	1915	1915	Us.	—	Astra Torres. Envelope to C.1, car to *Eta*
SS.1	18.3.15	7.5.15	Fire	—	Prototype, B.E.2c car ↓
SS.2	1915	1915	Us.	—	Willows
SS.3	1915	19.4.18	Us.	—	Short Bros., AEF
SS.4	1915	2.6.17	Sold	—	To Italy
SS.5	1915	2.6.17	Sold	—	To Italy
SS.6	1915	2.6.17	Sold	—	To Italy
SS.7	13.9.15	19.4.18	Us.	—	AEF
SS.8	1915	19.4.18	Us.	—	AEF
SS.9	1915	13.9.16	Us.	—	Replaced
SS.9A	3.2.17	15.6.18	Us.	—	—
SS.10	5.1915	10.9.15	Wrecked at sea	—	Replaced
SS.10A	1916	2.6.16	Us.	—	Replaced
SS.10B	2.6.17	2.6.17	Sold	—	To Italy
SS.11	1915	2.6.17	Sold	—	To Italy
SS.12	1915	14.3.16	Us.	—	—
SS.13/SS.14A	1915	9.1919	* Us.	—	Renumbered 13.10.17
SS.14	1915	1.5.18	Us.	—	—
SS.15	9.8.15	18.1.17	Wrecked	—	Off Lundy Is.
SS.16	1915	11.5.18	Us.	—	—
SS.17	1915	19.4.18	Us.	—	AEF
SS.18	26.9.15	9.11.16	Wrecked at sea	—	One dead
SS.19	1915	19.4.18	Us.	—	AEF
SS.20	1915	17.7.18	Us.	—	—

Designation number	Delivery date	Deletion or transfer date	Reason	Hours flown	Details
SS.21	1915	1915	Sold	—	To France
SS.22	5.11.15	2.6.17	Sold	—	To Italy
SS.23	1915	1.5.18	Us.	—	—
SS.24	1915	17.7.18	Us.	—	—
SS.25	1915	15.3.18	Us.	—	—
SS.26	17.12.15	28.12.15	Sold	—	To France
SS.27	18.7.15	5.8.15	Wrecked	—	Whitworth car. Hit Marquise steeple.
SS.28	1915	12.3.18	Us.	17+	Farman car ↓ Replaced
SS.28A	1918	10.1919	* Us.	811+	—
SS.29	1915	9.1919	* Us.	568+	—
SS.30	1916	23.10.17	Us.	—	Replaced
SS.30A	12.1917	9.1919	* Us.	848	—
SS.31	1916	2.11.17	Us.	—	Replaced
SS.31A	2.1918	9.1919	* Us.	665	—
SS.32	1916	10.10.16	Us.	—	Replaced
SS.32A	10.1916	17.7.18	Us.	—	—
SS.33	1916	1917	Us.	—	—
SS.34	1916	5.5.17	Destroyed by gale	—	*Beta* car to 22.7.16, Farman 22.7.16 on
SS.35	1916	9.1919	* Us.	43	—
SS.36	1916	9.1.19	* Us.	—	—
SS.37	1916	14.1.18	Forced landing	168+	Replaced
SS.37A	6.1918	9.1919	* Us.	360	—
SS.38	1916	2.2.17	Lost at sea	—	—
SS.39	1916	30.9.17	Us.	—	Replaced
SS.39A	1.10.17	9.1919	* Us.	179	Whitworth car ↓
SS.40	6.7.16	1.10.18	Us.	—	Loaned RFC 1916, AEF
SS.41	3.7.16	11.5.18	Us.	—	—
SS.42	8.1916	4.10.16	Us.	—	Replaced
SS.42A	1917	12.9.17	Lost at sea	63	Two dead
SS.43	9.7.16	11.5.18	Us.	—	—
SS.44	1916	1916	Sold	—	To Italy
SS.45	1916	1916	Sold	—	To Italy
SS.46	1916	1916	Sold	—	To Italy
SS.47	1916	1916	Sold	—	To Italy
SS.48	1916	1916	Sold	—	BE2c car ↓ To France
SS.49	1916	1916	Sold	—	To France
SSP.1	31.1.17	9.1919	* Us.	370+	—
SSP.2	28.5.17	26.11.17	Lost at sea	63+	One dead
SSP.3	23.2.17	21.3.17	Wrecked	—	—
SSP.4	12.6.17	21.12.17	Lost at sea	165+	Three dead
SSP.5	18.6.17	9.1919	* Us.	391+	—
SSP.6	16.6.17	9.1919	* Us.	316+	—

Designation number	Delivery date	Deletion or transfer date	Reason	Hours flown	Details
SS.0/SSZ.1	9.1916	10.1919	* Us.	961	Prototype
SSZ.2	6.1917	14.8.17	Lost at sea	86	—
SSZ.3	6.1917	7.12.18	* Us.	269	—
SSZ.4	6.1917	10.1919	* Us.	1,198	—
SSZ.5	7.1917	17.9.18	Fire	1,266	—
SSZ.6	7.1917	10.1919	* Us.	1,033	—
SSZ.7	7.1917	20.12.17	Fire	376	Collision, one dead
SSZ.8	7.1917	10.1919	* Us.	1,214	—
SSZ.9	7.1917	22.1.19	* Us.	1,027	—
SSZ.10	8.1917	20.12.17	Fire	320	Collision
SSZ.11	7.1917	10.1919	* Us.	1,610	—
SSZ.12	7.1917	10.1919	* Us.	1,296	—
SSZ.13	8.1917	30.8.18	Wrecked at sea	1,132	—
SSZ.14	7.1917	10.1919	* Us.	831	—

SSZ.4 was commissioned in June, 1917, and based at Capel. She flew 1,198 hours in service before being deleted with so many other non-rigids in October, 1919. *Imperial War Museum*

Designation number	Delivery date	Deletion or transfer date	Reason	Hours flown	Details
SSZ.15	9.1917	13.4.18	Lost at sea	372	—
SSZ.16	8.1917	10.1919	* Us.	1,408	—
SSZ.17	8.1917	22.1.18	Fire	501	—
SSZ.18	9.1917	10.1919	* Us.	828	—
SSZ.19	10.1917	10.1919	* Us.	1,001	—
SSZ.20	10.1917	10.1919	* Us.	1,417	—
SSZ.21	9.1917	1917	Sold	—	To France
SSZ.22	9.1917	1917	Sold	—	To France
SSZ.23	1.1918	14.8.18	Sold	336	To USA
SSZ.24	11.1917	11.1917	Sold	—	To USA
SSZ.25	12.1917	4.2.18	Destroyed by gale	57	—
SSZ.26	1.1918	27.2.18	Lost at sea	90	—
SSZ.27	2.1918	10.1919	* Us.	782	—
SSZ.28	2.1918	10.1919	* Us.	932	—
SSZ.29	2.1918	10.1919	* Us.	871	—
SSZ.30	2.1918	10.1919	* Us.	794	—

The first of a type based on the Mullion Twin, SST.1 was stationed at Capel and flew 159 hours in service after being commissioned in June, 1918. Had the war not ended there would have been 115 of these twin-engined airships in service by the middle of 1919. *Fleet Air Arm Museum*

Designation number	Delivery date	Deletion or transfer date	Reason	Hours flown	Details
SSZ.31	3.1918	24.1.19	* Us.	323	—
SSZ.32	3.1918	10.1919	* Us.	246	—
SSZ.33	3.1918	22.1.19	* Us.	553	—
SSZ.34	3.1918	26.11.18	* Us.	860	—
SSZ.35	3.1918	17.10.18	Lost at sea	822	—
SSZ.36	4.1918	10.1919	* Us.	644	—
SSZ.37	4.1918	10.1919	* Us.	675	—
SSZ.38	4.1918	16.8.18	Fire	48	—
SSZ.39	4.1918	29.1.19	* Us.	856	—
SSZ.40	4.1918	10.1919	* Us.	463	—
SSZ.41	4.1918	28.1.19	* Us.	760	—
SSZ.42	4.1918	10.1919	* Us.	579	—
SSZ.43	5.1918	10.1919	* Us.	566	—
SSZ.44	5.1918	10.1919	* Us.	373	—
SSZ.45	5.1918	10.1919	* Us.	503	—
SSZ.46	5.1918	10.1919	* Us.	648	—
SSZ.47	5.1918	10.1919	* Us.	380	—
SSZ.48	5.1918	10.1919	* Us.	553	—
SSZ.49	5.1918	2.9.18	Lost at sea	349	—
SSZ.50	3.1918	24.1.19	* Us.	775	—
SSZ.51	3.1918	15.8.18	Lost at sea	655	—
SSZ.52	3.1918	10.1919	* Us.	702	—
SSZ.53	3.1918	10.1919	* Us.	917	—
SSZ.54	4.1918	16.8.18	Fire	201	—
SSZ.55	6.1918	10.1919	* Us.	153	—
SSZ.56	4.1918	10.1919	* Us.	539	—
SSZ.57	4.1918	10.1919	* Us.	261	—
SSZ.58	4.1918	10.1919	* Us.	397	—
SSZ.59	4.1918	10.1919	* Us.	174	—
SSZ.60	4.1918	21.1.19	* Us.	195	—
SSZ.61	5.1918	2.1.19	* Us.	320	—
SSZ.62	5.1918	1.1919	* Us.	69	—
SSZ.63	5.1918	10.1919	* Us.	110	—
SSZ.64	5.1918	10.1919	* Us.	325	—
SSZ.65	5.1918	10.1919	* Us.	252	—
SSZ.66	5.1918	10.1919	* Us.	159	—
SSZ.67	5.1919	10.1919	* Us.	639	—
SSZ.68	8.1918	—	* —	—	AEF
SSZ.69	6.1918	10.1919	* Us.	495	—
SSZ.70	8.1918	—	* —	—	AEF
SSZ.71	12.1918	10.1919 △	Us.	8	—
SSZ.72	11.1918	10.1919	* Us.	55	—
SSZ.73	9.1918	10.1919	* Us.	237	—
SSZ.74	11.1918	10.1919	* Us.	30	—
SSZ.75	11.1918	10.1919	* Us.	43	—
SSZ.76	11.1918	10.1919 △	Us.	13	—
SSZ.77	1.1919	10.1919 △	Us.	5	—

Designation number	Delivery date	Deletion or transfer date	Reason	Hours flown	Details
SSE.1	2.5.18	9.7.18	Us.	4	—
SSE.2	3.1918	10.1919 *	Us.	57	"Mullion Twin"
SSE.3	3.1919	1921 △	Us.	105+	—
SST.1	6.1918	7.4.19 *	Us.	159	—
SST.2	7.1918	28.1.19 *	Us.	91	—
SST.3	7.1918	18.6.19 *	Us.	191	—
SST.4	8.1918	10.1919 *	Us.	189	—
SST.5	8.1918	5.11.18	Destroyed by gale	196	—
SST.6	29.8.18	30.8.18	Fire	—	Not accepted; crashed on maiden flight, five dead
SST.7	9.1918	1.1919 *	Us.	101	—
SST.8	10.1918	1.1919 *	Us.	94	—
SST.9	10.1918	6.1919 *	Sold	98	To USA
SST.10	10.1918	9.6.19 *	Us.	115	—
SST.11	10.1918	6.1919 *	Sold	38	To USA
SST.12	10.1918	6.1919 *	Sold	39	To USA
SST.14	5.1919	10.1919 △	Us.	55	—
C.1	16.1.16	1.6.18	Us.	—	—
C.2	28.1.16	10.1919 *	Us.	2,273	—
C.3	9.6.16	31.8.18	Us.	405+	—
C.4	7.1916	10.9.19 *	Us.	1,478	Replacement of earlier C.4
C.5	16.6.16	30.1.17	Crashed	—	Car replaced
C.5A	8.1917	10.1919 *	Us.	880	—
C.6	7.1916	24.3.17	Lost at sea	—	—
C.7	7.1916	1.10.18	Us.	774	—
C.8	16.5.16	9.6.16	Lost at sea	—	Three dead
C.9	7.1916	1.10.18	Us.	2,500	—
C.10	8.1916	10.10.16	Us.	—	Replaced
C.10A	8.1917	17.7.18	Us.	345	—
C.11	6.1916	12.3.18	Us.	—	Four dead
C.12	6.1916	12.3.18	Us.	—	Car to C*1
C.13/C.14A	1.1917	10.1919 *	Us.	35+	Renumbered 11.1917
C.14	9.1916	17.7.18	Us.	496	—
C.15	23.8.16	16.7.17	Wrecked	—	—
C.16	8.1916	14.9.16	Wrecked	—	—
C.17	8.1916	21.4.17	Shot down	—	Five dead
C.18	11.1916	31.8.18	Us.	291	—
C.19	11.9.16	31.8.18	Us.	420	—
C.20	23.9.16	22.12.17	Lost at sea	110+	—
C.21	26.9.16	2.6.18	Us.	438	—
C.22	9.1916	21.3.17	Lost at sea	—	—

C.4 was one of only four Coastal airships still in service at the Armistice. Commissioned in July, 1916, as a replacement for an earlier C.4 which had been sold to France, she survived until October, 1919.

Fleet Air Arm Museum

Designation number	Delivery date	Deletion or transfer date	Reason	Hours flown	Details
C.23	24.10.16	11.7.17	Wrecked	—	Replaced
C.23A	9.1917	10.5.18	Wrecked	900	One dead
C.24	12.1916	4.4.18	Us.	260	—
C.25	10.1916	31.7.18	Lost at sea	716	Five dead
C.26	21.11.16	13.12.17	Interned	202	In Holland
C.27	16.12.16	11.12.17	Shot down	355	Five dead
C.a	1916	1916	Sold	—	To Russia
C.b	1916	1916	Sold	—	To Russia
C.c	1916	1916	Sold	—	To Russia
C.d	1916	1916	Sold	—	To Russia
C.e	23.4.16	1916	Sold	—	To France Originally C.4
C*1	2.1918	10.1919	* Us.	868	—
C*2	3.1918	10.1919	* Us.	561	—
C*3	4.1918	10.1919	* Us.	588	—
C*4	5.1918	10.1919	* Us.	509	—
C*5	5.1918	10.1919	* Us.	537	—
C*6	5.1918	10.1919	* Us.	523	—
C*7	6.1918	10.1919	* Us.	331	—
C*8	7.1918	10.1919	* Us.	204	—
C*9	7.1918	10.1919	* Us.	164	—
C*10	7.1918	10.1919	* Us.	656	—

Designation number	Delivery date	Deletion or transfer date	Reason		Hours flown	Details
NS.1	2.1917	22.2.18		Wrecked	207	—
NS.2	6.1917	22.2.18		Wrecked	11	—
NS.3	7.1917	22.6.18		Lost at sea	647	Five dead
NS.4	10.1917	10.1919	*	Us.	265	—
NS.5	12.1917	22.2.18		Wrecked	14	—
NS.6	5.1918	10.1919	*	Us.	398	—
NS.7	6.1918	1921	*	Us.	450	—
NS.8	7.1918	10.1919	*	Us.	281	—
NS.9	7.1918	3.10.18		Us.	152	—
NS.10	8.1918	3.10.18		Us.	128	—
NS.11	9.1918	15.7.19	*	Lightning	492	Ten dead
NS.12	10.1918	10.1919	*	Us.	95	—
NS.14	8.11.18	8.11.18		Sold	—	To USA
NS.16	3.1919	10.1919	△	Us.	89	—

NS.4 after being rebuilt to correct the problems posed by the complex drive to the propellers. At the same time the fuel tanks, which had been placed externally above the side lobes of the envelope, were fitted inside the envelope to improve streamlining and weight distribution.   *Imperial War Museum*

Designation number	Delivery date	Deletion or transfer date	Reason	Hours flown	Details
No 5	11.1917	9.7.18	Spares	107	Parseval, Coastal car
No 6	12.1915	10.1919 *	Us.	406	Parseval
No 7	12.1917	28.3.18	Spares	8	Parseval
SR.1	11.1918	20.9.19 *	Us.	122	Semi-rigid
No 9	4.4.17	28.6.18	Us.	198	First rigid to fly
No 23	15.10.17	9.1919 *	Us.	321	—
No 24	28.10.17	12.1919 *	Us.	165	—
No 25	14.10.17	9.1919 *	Us.	221	—
R.26	22.4.18	10.3.1919 *	Us.	198	—
R.27	29.6.18	16.8.18	Fire	90	One dead
R.29	20.6.18	24.10.19 *	Us.	438	—
R.31	6.11.18	7.1919 *	Us.	5	—
R.32	9.1919	1921 △	Us.	212+	—
R.33	6.1919	1928 △	Us.	800	—
R.34	5.1919	1.1921 △	Wrecked	329	—
R.36	4.1921	1926 △	Us.	80	—
R.38	6.1921	23.8.21 △	Broke up in mid-air	56	Forty-four dead
R.80	7.1920	9.1921 △	Us.	73	—

Us. = Unserviceable or no longer required.
AEF= Airship Expeditionary Force.
*= In service 11/11/18
△= Delivered post-war

The official records are incomplete, particularly for the first two years of the war. The delivery date given above is usually that of joining the air station, but can be either the first service flight or an approximate date. Airships were normally commissioned on the day of the delivery flight, but while most were flown to their station, some arrived by rail and had to be assembled. There are other problems to exact dating; SSZ.72, for example, left Kingsnorth before Armistice Day for Anglesey, but flew in stages by way of Cranwell and Howden, and consequently did not reach her station until 12th November. She has been taken to be a wartime airship, as has R.31, which left Cardington before the Armistice but never reached her official station at all. The number of hours flown is in service. Deletion was usually immediate upon the loss of the airship, but official acknowledgement was frequently delayed. A repaired airship normally retained her original designation; one which was extensively renovated was usually given an A suffix and regarded as a replacement. Of those airships sold, some were transferred immediately upon commission, others only after long service.

British Military Airship Classes 1914–1921

Type	Total number	Not accepted	Sold during war	Deleted before 11/11/18	In Service 11/11/18	Delivered post-war
Willows	1	0	0	1	0	0
Beta	1	0	0	1	0	0
Gamma	1	0	0	1	0	0
Delta	1	0	0	1	0	0
Eta	1	0	0	1	0	0
Astra Torres	3	0	0	3	0	0
SS	59	0	14	36	9	0
SSP	6	0	0	3	3	0
SSZ	77	0	4	14	56	3
SST	13	1	0	1	10	1
SSE	3	0	0	1	1	1
Coastal	35	0	5	26	4	0
C Star	10	0	0	0	10	0
North Sea	14	0	1	6	6	1
Parseval	4	0	0	3	1	0
SR.1	1	0	0	0	1	0
Rigid	14	0	0	2	6	6
	244	1	24	100	107	12

Three of the SS Twins were sold postwar to the USA, as was R.38. Four uncommissioned SS airships were sold privately by Vickers.

Select Bibliography

Abbott, P. *Airship: The story of R.34 and the first east-west crossing of the Atlantic by air.* Adams and Dart, 1973.

Chamberlain, G. *Airships Cardington: A history of Cardington airship station and its role in world airship development.* Terence Dalton, 1984.

Davey, M. J. B. *Interpretive History of Flight.* HMSO, 1948.

Gamble, C. F. S. *The Story of a North Sea Air Station.* Oxford University Press, 1928; Neville Spearman, 1967.

Gilpin, B. J. "The Coastal Airship." *Cross and Cockade*, vol 15, 1984.

Grey, C. G., ed. *Jane's All The World's Aircraft.* Sampson, Low, Marston and Co., 1919; reprinted, David and Charles, 1969.

Higham, R. *The British Rigid Airship 1908–1931.* G. T. Foulis, 1961.

Jackson, R. *Airships.* Cassell, 1971.

Kinsey, G. *Pulham Pigs: The history of an airship station.* Terence Dalton, 1988.

Lewis, P. *British Aircraft, 1809–1914.* Putnam, 1962.

McKinty, A. *The Father of British Airships. A Biography of E. T. Willows.* William Kimber, 1972.

Meager, G. *My Airship Flights.* William Kimber, 1970.

Morpurgo, J. *Barnes Wallis.* Longman, 1972.

Raleigh, W. and Jones, A. H. *The War in the Air.* Clarendon Press, 6 volumes, 1922 on.

Robinson, D. *The Zeppelin in Combat.* G. T. Foulis, 1966.

Robinson, D. *Giants in the Sky: A History of the Rigid Airship.* G. T. Foulis, 1971.

Roskill, S. W., ed. *Documents relating to the Naval Air Service.* Navy Records Society, 1969.

Saunders, A. "The Polegate Airship Disaster." *Wingspan*, March/April, 1989.

Ventry and Kolesnik, E. M. *Airship Saga.* Blandford Press, 1982.

Williams, T. B. *Airship Pilot No 28.* William Kimber, 1974.

Original Sources

Public Record Office:

AIR 1/727/152/5	The SS airship
	The Coastal airship
	The C Star airship
	The North Sea airship
	The work of the non-rigid airship through the war
	(Contemporary unpublished accounts)
AIR 1/2315/222/6/A	History and Record of Airships
	(Contemporary official register, with details)
AIR 2/190/MR1588	Report of R.29's attack on U-boat
AIR 1/720/42/1/1	Report of SSZ.16's attack on U-boat
AIR 2/42/608043/17	Ditto
AIR 1/720/42/1/2	Lieutenant Monk's report on SS.42
AIR 1/652/17/122/478	Report on SS.40 in France
AIR 2/168/MR/909	Disposal of Airships (Airships in store)

Handbook of SS Airships, Admiralty, 1917
Handbook of Airship No 23, Admiralty, 1918
Handbook of Airship No 9, Admiralty, 1918
Handbook of Coastal and C Star Airships, Admiralty, 1918
Article in *The Times*, 12th July, 1919
Article in *Flight* magazine, 21st August, 1919
Article in *Aeroplane* magazine, 20th August, 1919
Many small items from PRO documents, *Flight* and *The Times*, 1912–1919

Index

Illustrations in bold type

Index of Airships

Western Approaches

Towards Cherbourg

Research by Norman Peake
Drawn by Paul Maister

S.S. Patrols usually
sighted each other

NS.11 Lost

C.17 Shot Down

C.27 Shot Down